Tatui Baba

An Elementary Grammar of the Japanese Language

With Easy Progressive Exercises. Second Edition

Tatui Baba

An Elementary Grammar of the Japanese Language
With Easy Progressive Exercises. Second Edition

ISBN/EAN: 9783337085384

Printed in Europe, USA, Canada, Australia, Japan

Cover: Foto ©Paul-Georg Meister /pixelio.de

More available books at **www.hansebooks.com**

AN

ELEMENTARY GRAMMAR

OF THE

JAPANESE LANGUAGE,

WITH

Easy Progressive Exercises.

BY

TATUI BABA.

SECOND AND ENLARGED EDITION.

LONDON:
TRÜBNER AND CO., 57 & 59, LUDGATE HILL.

NEW YORK:
D. APPLETON AND CO., 1, 3 & 5, BOND STREET.

1888.

LONDON:
PRINTED BY GILBERT AND RIVINGTON, LIMITED,
ST. JOHN'S HOUSE, CLERKENWELL ROAD.

TO

THE RIGHT HONOURABLE

THE LORD HOUGHTON,

THIS BOOK IS RESPECTFULLY DEDICATED BY

THE AUTHOR.

PREFACE TO THE SECOND EDITION.

WHEN this book was published in 1873, the object was twofold. The first was to protest against an idea entertained by some of my countrymen that the Japanese language is very imperfect, and therefore it must be exterminated. This idea, however, appears to have been given up as altogether preposterous and extravagant. The second was to give a general idea of the Japanese language as it is spoken. Maturer thought suggests to me some alterations, but I found that no material change is necessary. I have added several new Exercises which I deemed advisable, and trusting that in its new form it will prove acceptable, I have the pleasure of submitting a second edition of the work.

THE AUTHOR.

NEW YORK,
    January, 1888.

JAPANESE GRAMMAR.

I. THE ALPHABET,

OR

THE IROHA.

THE letters used in Japanese are forty-seven. They have two different forms, one of which is called *Katakana*, and the other *Hirakana*. We give the *Katakana*, as under:—

イ ロ ハ ニ ホ ヘ ト チ リ ヌ ヲ ク
カ ヨ タ レ ソ ツ子 ナ ラ ム ウ ヰ ノ
オ ク ヤ マ ケ フ コ エ テ ア サ キ ユ
メ ミ シ ヱ ヒ モ セ ス

These letters are called in Japanese:—

i ro ha ni ho he to ti ri nu ru o wa' ka yo ta re so tu ne na ra mu u i no o ku ya ma ke fu ko ye te a sa ki yu me mi si ye hi mo se zu.

The whole system of the letters is called Iroha, from イ ロ ハ, the names of these first three letters.

2. THE VOWELS.

Of the above forty-seven, five (ア イ ウ エ ヲ) are vowels; the sounds of these five letters are as follows :—

 a ア has the sound of *a* in master, or mama.
 i イ ,, ,, *i* in inland.
 u ウ ,, ,, *u* in queen.
 e エ ,, ,, *e* in echo.
 o ヲ ,, ,, *o* in month.

The rest of the letters are arranged according to these five vowels, as follows :—

a	ア	i	イ	u	ウ	e	エ	o	ヲ
ka	カ	ki	キ	ku	ク	ke	ケ	ko	コ
sa	サ	si	シ	su	ス	se	セ	so	ソ
ta	タ	ti	チ	tu	ツ	te	テ	to	ト
na	ナ	ni	ニ	nu	ヌ	ne	子	no	ノ
ha	ハ	hi	ヒ	fu	フ	he	ヘ	ho	ホ
ma	マ	mi	ミ	mu	ム	me	メ	mo	モ
ya	ヤ	yi	イ	yu	ユ	ye	エ	yo	ヨ
ra	ラ	ri	リ	ru	ル	re	レ	ro	ロ
wa	ワ	wi	ヰ	wu	ウ	we	エ	wo	ヲ

Etymology.

When the sign ° or ＂ is marked on the head of a letter, as ガ or パ, it changes its sound; カ (*ka*) becomes ガ (*ga*), and ハ (*ha*), パ (*pa*). These changes will be seen in the following table :—

ga	ガ	gi	ギ	gu	グ	ge	ゲ	go	ゴ
za	ザ	zi	ジ	zu	ズ	ze	ゼ	zo	ゾ
da	ダ	di	ヂ	du	ヅ	de	デ	do	ド
ba	バ	bi	ビ	bu	ブ	be	ベ	bo	ボ
pa	パ	pi	ピ	pu	プ	pe	ペ	po	ポ

ヱ and エ, イ and ヰ, オ and ヲ, are distinguished by ancient usage, but at the present time the distinction is no longer observed.

In most parts of Japan, ヂ *di* and ジ *zi*, ヅ *du* and ズ *zu*, are distinguished from one another in their pronunciation, although they are pronounced alike in some parts of the country.

II. THE PARTS OF SPEECH.

Words are divided into eight classes, that is, parts of speech—Nouns, Adjectives, Pronouns, Verbs, Adverbs, Postpositions, Conjunctions, and Interjections.

Note—There is nothing in Japanese to answer to the English Articles, definite or indefinite.

Of Nouns.

A Noun is the name of any person, place, or thing; as, *niwa* garden; *Nipon*, Japan.

Nouns are either Proper or Common :—

1. A Proper Noun is the name of any particular person, place, or thing, as Yokohama, Kosi.

2. A Common Noun is a name given in common to everything of the same kind, as *tukuye*, table.

Nouns are varied by number and gender.

Of Number.

There are two numbers, the Singular and the Plural.

In Japanese, nouns change their forms in a few cases; generally they have the same forms, both in the plural and singular. But when they change their forms the plural is rendered by adding *domo, gata,* or *ra* to the singular; as *ko*, child; *danna*, gentleman; *shosei*, student, in the singular; and *kodomo, dannagata, shoseira*, in the plural.

The number of nouns generally are distinguished by numeral adjectives; as, *hito hitori*, one person; *hito futari*, two persons.

Of Gender.

Nouns have three genders—the Masculine, Feminine, and Neuter.

Of Gender.

The masculine denotes the male sex; as, *otoko*, man. The feminine denotes the female sex; as *onna*, woman. The neuter denotes whatever is without sex; as, *yama*, mountain.

There are two different ways of distinguishing the sex:—

1. By different words; as—

Masculine.	*Feminine.*
otoko, man.	*onna*, woman.
teishu, husband.	*niyobo*, wife.
sō, monk.	*ama*, nun.
goke, widow. [*yamome*, widower.]	*yamome*, widower.
segare, son.	*musume*, daughter.
titi, father.	*haha*, mother.
oji, uncle.	*oba*, aunt.
oi, nephew.	*mei*, niece.
hana muko, bridegroom.	*hana yome*, bride.
danna, gentleman.	*fuzin*, lady.

2. By prefixing another word; as—

Masculine.	*Feminine.*
otoko no ko, male child.	*onna no ko*, female child.
ontori, male bird.	*mentori*, female bird.
Tei, Emperor.	*Niyotei*, Empress.
Ō, King.	*Niyo-ō*, Queen.

Of Case.

There are three cases; namely, the Nominative, Possessive, and Objective.

The nominative is rendered by placing the sign *wa, ga,* or *mo* after nouns; as, *otoko* ga or wa, mo, *ikimasu,* man goes.

The possessive is formed by putting the sign *no* after nouns; as, *otoko* no *kimono,* man's dress.

The objective is rendered by the sign *wo, ni,* or *ga*— *Otoko ga onna* wo *utimasita,* A man has beaten a woman. In the potential mood, *ga* is used as a sign of the objective case.

> *Note*—The signs of the nominative, *wa* and *mo* are used in opposition to each other. When two things or persons do the same actions, *mo* is used; as, *Onna* mo *otoko* mo *ikimasu,* Both man and woman go. But when they do some different actions, *wa* is used; as, *Onna* wa *kayerimasu ga* (but) *otoko* wa *orimasu,* Woman goes away, but man stays.
>
> *Ga* is sometimes used in an emphatic sentence; as, *Watakusi* ga *simasita,* I have done it.
>
> *Ni,* the sign of the objective case, answers to the dative in Latin; and in English it may be translated into 'to,' or 'for;' as *Kane wo otoko* ni *yare,* Give money to the man.

Of Adjectives.

An adjective is a word which qualifies a noun.

Of Pronouns.

Adjectives have three degrees of comparison—the Positive, Comparative, and Superlative.

The comparative is formed by placing *yori* or *yorimo* (more than) before the positive; as, *yori yoi*, better; and the superlative by putting the words *ichi ban*, or *mottomo*, before the positive; as, *itti ban*, or *mottomo yoi*, best.

There are three kinds of adjectives, namely, qualificative, quantitative, and demonstrative:—

1. Qualificative adjectives express the quality; as, *kireina shomotu*, fine books.

2. Quantitative adjectives express the quantity; as, *takusanna shomotu*, many books.

3. Demonstrative adjectives serve to point out; as, *kono shomotu*, this book; *sono shomotu*, that book.

Of Pronouns.

A Pronoun is a word used instead of a Noun. There are three kinds of pronouns—Personal, Interrogative, and Demonstrative.

Note—Relative Pronouns are not used in conversation.

1. Personal Pronouns are used to represent the three persons, namely, first, second, and third person. They have numbers and cases, but they are applied both to feminine and masculine without distinction.

Of Interrogative Pronouns.

The whole of the personal pronouns in their simple forms may be represented thus :—

	First Person.	Second Person.	Third Person.
Singular.	*watakusi,*	*anata,* ga	*are,* or *kare.*
Plural	*watakusi domo,*	*anatagata,*	*arera,* or *karera.*

The cases are rendered by placing *ni, no,* and the other particles after pronouns, as in cases of *watakusi ga,* or *wa,* I; *watakusi ni,* me.

Are and *arera* are seldom used in conversation. Generally the names of persons are repeated, or else demonstrative adjectives and *hito* or *okata* (person) are used; as, *Kono* okata *ga ikimasu,* This person goes.

2. Interrogative Pronouns are used to ask questions.

There are three kinds of interrogative pronouns— *dare,* which is applied to persons; *nani,* which is applied to things, or inferior animals; and *dore,* which is used when a choice is expressed.

The cases are rendered by the particles *no, ni, wa,* and the others as in case of a noun. Examples:— *Sokoni* dare *ga imasu ka?* Who is there? *Sokoni* nani *ga imasu ka?* What is there? Dore *wo anata wa torimasu ka?* Which do you take?

> *Note*—When any question is asked, the sign *ka* is always put at the end of the sentence.

3. Demonstrative Pronouns serve to point out the object spoken of.

Of Verbs.

There are two kinds of demonstrative pronouns, namely, *kore* and *sore*, which correspond to 'this' and 'that' in English. They have cases, which are rendered like cases of a noun: they have the same forms both in the plural and singular. Examples:— Kore *wo ō-torinasare*, Take this; *Watakusi ni* sore *wo kudasare*, Give me that.

OF VERBS.

A Verb is a word used to express existence or action. Verbs are of three kinds—Active, Passive, and Neuter.

1. An Active Verb expresses action passing from an actor to some object; as, *Watakusi wa shomotu wo mimasu*, I see or read a book.

2. A Passive Verb expresses the suffering of an action performed by another; as, *Watakusi wa hito ni** *miraremasu*, I am seen by people.

3. A Neuter Verb is *neither* active nor passive; it expresses existence, condition of being, and action limited to the actor; as, *Watakusi wa nemurimasu*, I sleep.

Inflection of Verbs.

Verbs are inflected to express voices, moods, and tenses. There are three kinds of Japanese verbs—first,

---

* Here *ni* means 'by' in English.

utu, to strike; second, *nageru,* to throw; third, *suru,* to do, or make.

1. *Active Voice.*

When the verbs are used in conversation, *u* of the verbs of the first kind is substituted by *i,* and *masu* in an affirmative sentence, or *masen* in a negative sentence is added, as *utimasu* or *utimasen; ru* of that of the second is taken away, and *masu* or *masen* is put, as *nagemasu* or *nagemasen; uru* of that of the third is substituted by *i,* and *masu* or *masen* is added, as *simasu* or *simasen.*

2. *Passive Voice.*

In the case of passive voices, *u* of the verb of the first kind is substituted by *are,* and *masu* or *masen;* as, *Utare masu,* Are or is beaten. This rule applies to the verbs of the second kind; as, *Nagerare masu,* Is or are thrown down. *Uru* of that of the third kind is substituted by *erare,* and *masu* or *masen* is added; as, *Kerai ni serare masu,* He is, or they are, made a servant or servants.

Of Moods.

Verbs have five moods—the Indicative, Potential, Subjunctive, Imperative, and Infinitive.

1. The Indicative Mood is the simple affirmation of a fact; as, *Watakusi ga* mimasu, I see (it).
2. The Potential Mood expresses the power of doing

Conjugation of Verbs. 11

an action; as, *Watakusi wa sore ga* miyemusu, or *Watakusi wa sore wo* miru koto ga dekimasu, I can see it or that.

3. The Subjunctive Mood represents a thing under a condition, and is preceded by a conjunction (*mosi*), and followed by another conjunction (*nara* or *naraba*); as, Moshi *anata ga ikimasu* nara, If you go. Sometimes the word *mosi* is omitted; as, *Anata ga ikimasu* nara, If you go.

4. The Imperative Mood commands or entreats, as, *Miyo* or *Mite-kudasare*, See, or Pray see.

5. The Infinitive Mood expresses an action without regard to persons or numbers; as, *Miru koto*, To see.

Of Tenses.

Verbs have three tenses—the Present, the Past, and the Future.

1. The Present Tense expresses what is going on at present; as, *Watakusi ga* yomimasu, I read, or am reading.

2. The Past Tense represents an action as finished; as, *Watakusi wa kono shomotu wo* yomimasita, I have read, or I read this book.

3. The Future Tense represents an action which is yet to be done; as, *Watakusi wa* yomimasho, I shall read.

CONJUGATION OF VERBS.

Verbs are divided into three classes. These are distin-

Conjugation of Regular Verbs.

guished by the termination of the present infinitive. The first ends in *u*, as *suku*, to like; the second ends in *ru*, as *kangayeru*, to think; the third ends in *uru*, as *suru*, to make.

Conjugation of Regular Verbs.

First Conjugation ending in U—*Iku*, To go.

Indicative Mood.

Present Tense.

Watakusi wa ik-imasu, I go.
Anata wa ik-imasu, you go.
Are wa ik-imasu, he or she goes.

Watakusi domo wa ik-imasu, we go.
Anatagata wa ik-imasu, you go.
Arera wa ik-imasu, they go.

Past Tense.

Watakusi wa ik-imasita, I went or have gone.
Anata wa ik-imasita, you went or have gone.
Are wa ik-imasita, he went, or has gone.

Watakusi domo wa ik-imasita, we went.
Anatagata wa ik-imasita, you went.
Arera wa ik-imasita, they went.

Future Tense.

Watakusi wa ik-imasho, I shall go.
Anata wa ik-imasho, you will go.
Are wa ik-imasho, he or she will go.

Watakusi domo wa ik-imasho, we shall go.
Anatagata wa ik-imasho, you will go.
Arera wa ik-imasho, they will go.

Conjugation of Regular Verbs.

Potential Mood.

Present Tense.

Watakusi wa ik-emasu, I can go.
Anata wa ik-emasu, you can go.
Are wa ik-emasu, he can go.

Watakusi domo wa ik-emasu, we can go.
Anatagata wa ik-emasu, you can go.
Arera wa ik-emasu, they can go.

Past Tense.

Watakui wa ik-emasita, I could go.
Anata wa ik-emasita, you could go.
Are wa ik-emasita, he could go.

Watakusi domo wa ik-emasita, we could go.
Anatagata wa ik-emasita, you could go.
Arera wa ik-emasita, they could go.

Future Tense.

Watakusi wa ik-emasho, I shall be able to go.
Anata wa ik-emasho, you will be able to go.
Are wa ik-emasho, he will be able to go.

Watakusi domo wa ik-emasho, we shall be able to go.
Anatagata wa ik-emasho, you will be able to go.
Arera wa ik-emasho, they will be able to go.

Subjunctive Mood.

Present Tense.

Mosi watakusi ga ik-imasu nara, if I go.
Mosi anata ga ik-imasu nara, if you go.
Mosi are ga ik-imasu nara, if he or she go.

Mosi watakusi domo ga ik-imasu nara, if we go.
Mosi anatagata ga ik-imasu nara, if you go.
Mosi arera ga ik-imasu nara, if they go.

Conjugation of Regular Verbs.

Past Tense.

Mosi watakusi ga ik-imasita nara, if I went, or have gone.

Mosi anata ga ik-imasita nara, if you went, or have gone.

Mosi are ga ik-imasita nara, if he went, or has gone.

Mosi watakusi domo ga ik-imasita nara, if we went, or have gone.

Mosi anatagata ga ik-imasita nara, if you went, or have gone.

Mosi arera ga ik-imasita nara, if they went, or have gone.

Imperative Mood.

Command .... *Ike,*

Entreaty ... { *I-tte-okure,* / *I-tte-kudasare,* } Go.

Infinitive Mood.

Iku koto, To go.

The same form of verbs is used for all the persons, singular or plural; so, hereafter, the verbs for the first persons only will be repeated.

Second Conjugation ending in RU—*Miru*, to see.

Indicative Mood.
Present Tense.

1. *Watakusi wa mi-masu,* I see.
2. . . . . .
3. . . . . .

1. *Watakusi domo wa mi-masu,* we see.
2. . . . . .
3. . . . . .

Past Tense.

1. *Watakusi wa mi-masita,* I saw, or have seen.
2. . . . . .
3. . . . . .

1. *Watakusi domo wa mi-masita,* we saw, or have seen.
2. . . . . .
3. . . . . .

Conjugation of Regular Verbs. 15

Future Tense.

1. *Watakusi wa mi-masho,* I shall see.
2. . . .
3. . . .

1. *Wakusi domo wa mi-masho,* we shall see.
2. . . .
3. . . .

Potential Mood.
Present Tense.

1. *Watakusi wa miru koto ga dekimasu,* I can see.
2. . . .
3. . . .

1. *Watakusi domo wa miru koto ga dekimasu,* we can see.
2. . . .
3. . . .

Past Tense.

1. *Watakusi wa miru koto ga dekimasita,* I could see.
2. . . .
3. . . .

1. *Watakusi domo wa miru koto ga dekimasita,* we could see.
2. . . .
3. . . .

Future Tense.

1. *Watakusi wa miru koto ga dekimasho,* I shall be able to see.
2. . . .
3. . . .

1. *Watakusi domo wa miru koto ga dekimasho,* we shall be able to see.
2. . . .
3. . . .

Subjunctive Mood.
Present Tense.

1. *Mosi watakusi ga mimasu nara,* if I see.
2. . . .
3. . . .

1. *Mosi watakusi domo ga mimasu nara,* if we see.
2. . . .
3. . . .

Conjugation of Regular Verbs.

Past Tense.

1. *Mosi watakusi ga mimasita nara,* if I saw, or have seen.
2. . . . . .
3. . . . . .

1. *Mosi watakusi domo ga mimasita nara,* if we saw, or have seen.
2. . . . . .
3. . . . . .

Imperative Mood.

Command .... *Miyo,*
Entreaty .... { *Mi-te-okure,* } See.
{ *Mi-te-kudasare,* }

Infinitive Mood.
Miru koto, to see.

Conjugation of Third Verb—*Kuru,* to come.

Indicative Mood.
Present Tense.

1. *Watakusi wa kimasu,* I come.
2. . . . . .
3. . . . . .

1. *Watakusi domo wa kimasu,* we come.
2. . . . . .
3. . . . . .

Past Tense.

1. *Watakusi wa kimasita,* I came.
2. . . . . .
3. . . . . .

1. *Watakusi domo wa kimasita,* we came.
2. . . . . .
3. . . . . .

Future Tense.

1. *Watakusi wa kimasho,* I shall come.
2. . . . . .
3. . . . . .

1. *Watakusi domo wa kimasho,* we shall come.
2. . . . . .
3. . . . . .

Conjugation of Regular Verbs.

Potential Mood.
Present Tense.

1. *Watakusi wa kuru koto ga dekimasu,* I can come.
2. . . . . .
3. . . . . .

1. *Watakusi domo wa kuru koto ga dekimasu,* we can come.
2. . . . . .
3. . . . . .

Past Tense.

1. *Watakusi wa kuru koto ga dekimasita,* I could come.
2. . . . . .
3. . . . . .

1. *Watakusi domo wa kuru koto ga dekimasita,* we could come.
2. . . . . .
3 . . . . .

Future Tense.

1. *Watakusi wa kuru koto ga dekimasho,* I shall be able to come.
2. . . . . .
3. . . . . .

1. *Watakusi domo wa kuru koto ga dekimasho,* we shall be able to come.
2. . . . . .
3. . . . . .

Subjunctive Mood.
Present Tense.

1. *Mosi watakusi ga kimasu nara,* if I come.
2. . . . . .
3. . . . . .

1. *Mosi watakusi domo ga kimasu nara,* if we come.
2. . . . . .
3. . . . . .

Past Tense.

1. *Mosi watakusi ga kimasita nara,* if I came.
2. . . . . .
3. . . . . .

1. *Mosi watakusi domo ga kimasita nara,* if we came.
2. . . . . .
3. . . . . .

Conjugation of Regular Verbs.

Imperative Mood.

Ki-te-okure, } Come.
Ki-te-kudasare,

Infinitive Mood.
Kuru koto, to come.

The Verb used Negatively.
Indicative Mood.
Present Tense.

1. *Watakusi wa ikimasen*, I do not go.
2. . . . . .
3. . . . . .

1. *Watakusi domo wa ikimasen*, we do not go.
2. . . . . .
3. . . . . .

Past Tense.

1. *Watakusi wa ikimasenanda*, I did not go.
2. . . . . .
3. . . . . .

1. *Watakusi domo wa ikimasenanda*, we did not go.
2. . . . . .
3. . . . . .

Future Tense.

1. *Watakusi wa ikimasumai*, I shall not go.
2. . . . . .
3. . . . . .

1. *Watakusi domo wa ikimasumai*, we shall not go.
2. . . . . .
3. . . . . .

Potential Mood.
Present Tense.

1. *Watakusi wa ikemasen*,* I cannot go.
2. . . . . .
3. . . . . .

1. *Watakusi domo wa ikemasen*, we cannot go.
2. . . . . .
3. . . . . .

* There is another form of potential mood—*iku koto ga dekimasen*.

Conjugation of Regular Verbs. 19

Past Tense.

1. *Watakusi wa ikemasen-anda*, I could not go.
2. . . . . .
3. . . . . .

1. *Watakusi domo wa ikemasenanda*, we could not go.
2. . . . . .
3. . . . . .

Future Tense.

1. *Watakusi wa ikemasumai*, I shall not be able to go.
2. . . . . .
3. . . . . .

1. *Watakusi domo wa ikemasumai*, we shall not be able to go.
2. . . . . .
3. . . . . .

Subjunctive Mood.
Present Tense.

1. *Mosi watakusi ga ikimasen nara*, if I do not go.
2. . . . . .
3. . . . . .

1. *Mosi watakusi domo ga ikimasen nara*, if we do not go.
2. . . . . .
3. . . . . .

Past Tense.

1. *Mosi watakusi ga ikimasenanda nara*, if I did not go.
2. . . . . .
3. . . . . .

1. *Mosi watakusi ga ikimasenanda nara*, if we did not go.
2. . . . . .
3. . . . . .

Imperative Mood.

Iku-na,
I-tte-kudasaruna, } Do not go.

Of Adverbs.

An Adverb is a word which qualifies a verb, an adjective, or other adverb; as, *kono kodomo wa shomotu wo yoku yomimasu,* These children read books well.

Adverbs may be divided into the following six classes:—

1. Adverbs of time—*ima,* now; *hayaku,* quickly; *sudeni,* already; *konniti,* to-day; *miyo-niti,* to-morrow; and others.
2. Adverbs of place—*sokoni,* there; *kokoni,* here; *tikaku,* nearly, &c.
3. Adverbs of quality; as, *yoku,* well; *kireini,* beautifully; *kitaini,* wonderfully, &c.
4. Adverbs of quantity—*sukosi,* little; *takusan,* much.
5. Adverbs of sequence or order—*dai-ittini,* firstly; *dai-nini,* secondly.
6. Adverbs of mood—*sayo,* just so; *hei,* yes; *zituni,* truly; *iye,* no, &c.

Of Postpositions.

A Postposition is a word put, in Japanese, *after* nouns and pronouns, to show the relation between them; as, *Watakusi wa Nipon kara France ni ikimasu,* I go from Japan to France.

Of Conjunctions.

A List of Postpositions.

Tameni, for; *wuyeni*, above; *atoni*, after; *utini*, within, or in; *mayeni* or *mayewo*, before; *aidani*, between; *sitani*, below; *hokani*, out of, or without; *tikani*, near; *hōni*, toward. (These are used with the article *no*; as, *iye no uchini*, in the house; *kuni no tameni*, for the country, or for the sake of the country.)— *Made*, into, or to; *mukatte*, against; *oite*, in. (These are used with *ni*; as, *London ni made*, to London.)— *Koyete*, beyond; *hanarete*, off; *nukete* or *tōsite*, through. (With *wo*; as, *mado wo nukete*, through the window.)— *Kara*, from; *ni* or *ye*, to; *made*, into; *to*, with; *nasini*, without;—without any additionl word; as, *London kara*, from London; *kono tokoro ni*, in this place.

Of Conjunctions.

A Conjunction is a word which joins words and sentences together; as, *Watakusi to kono ko ga Asakusa ye ikimasu,* I and this child go to Asakusa.

There are two kinds of conjunctions, namely, copulative and disjunctive.

1. Copulative conjunctions are—*momata*, also; *to*, and; *kara*, since; *naraba* or *nara*, if; *dakara*, therefore, &c.

2. Disjunctive conjunctions are—*keredomo*, although; *ga*, but; *sikasi*, yet; *aruiwa* or *matawa*, or; *yorimo*, than, &c.

Of Interjections.

An Interjection expresses some sudden wish or emotion of the mind; as, *Ā do itashimasho,* Ah! what shall I do?

The principal interjections are—*Ō, Ā, Ha-hā, Ho-i, Nasakenai, Oya-oya, Are, Naruhodo,* &c.

SYNTAX.

There are two kinds of sentences—simple and compound.

1. A simple sentence; as, *Kono hito wa kasikō gozarimasu,* He is clever.

2. A compound sentence; as, *Kono hito wa kasiko gozarimasu keredomo hatarakimasen,* He is clever, but he does not work.

Rules.

I. A verb must be put after its object; as, *Watakusi. we hana wo konomimasu,* I like flowers.

In this sentence the object *hana* is placed before the predicate *konomimasu.*

II. Prepositions are placed after nouns which they govern, and which are said to be in the objective case; as, *Watakusi wa* Yedo *ye mairimasu,* I go to Yedo.

Rules. 23

III When two or more nouns or pronouns are coupled with *to* (and), the signs of cases are put after the last nominative; as, *Watakusi to anata ga ikimasu,* I and you go.

IV. When two or more nouns or pronouns are connected by *matawa* (or), the particle *ka* is put immediately after the nouns or pronouns; as, *Watakusi* ka *matawa anata* ka *ga mairimasu,* I or you go.

V. Conjunctions couple the same tenses of verbs; as, *Watakusi wa sore wo* sukimasu *keredomo kore wo* kiraimasu, I like that, but (I) do not like or dislike this.

Conjunctions couple the same cases of nouns and pronouns; as, *Watakusi to anata ga ikimasu,* I and you go.

VI. One verb governs another in the infinitive mood; as, *Watakusi wa sake wo* nomu koto *wo konomimasen,* I do not like to drink *saké,* or spirit of rice.

When the verbs in the infinitive mood are governed by an active verb, or used as nouns, the signs of cases, *ga, wa,* or *wo,* are added to the simple forms of the verbs in the infinitive mood; as, *nomu koto wa,* or *nomu koto wo,* to drink. But when the verbs in the infinitive mood are governed by a neuter verb, *u* of the verb of the first kind, and *uru* of that of the third kind are taken away, and *i* and *ni* are added; in the case of the verbs of the second kind, *ru* is substituted by *ni*; as, *Watakusi wa* mini, or asobini *ikimasu*, I go to see (something), or to amuse myself. Here *u* of *asobu* and *ru* of *miru* are taken away, and *i* and *ni*, or *ni*, is put.

VII. When two nouns, or one pronoun and a noun come together, one signifying a possessor, and the other a thing possessed, the former is put in the possessive case; as, *Yamasiroya no shomotu*, Yamasiroya's book; or, *Anato no shomotu*, Your book.

VIII. When the verb *gozarimasu* or *arimasu* ('is' or 'are') is used, a noun or pronoun which comes immediately before the verbs requires the word *de* after it; as, *Watakusi wa Yamatoya de gozarimasu*, I am (Mr.) Yamatoya.

IX. Sentences which imply contingency and futurity require the subjunctive mood; as, Mosi *watakusi ga mairimasu* nara, or Mosi *watakusi ga mairimasho* nara, *Watakusi ga sore wo mimasho*, If I go (there), I shall see that.

X. Some conjunctions have their correspondent conjunctions; thus, *to* (and) is sometimes repeated after each noun or pronoun; as, *Watakusi* to *anata* to *ga ikimasu*, I and you go.

Rules. 25

Mosi .. .. *nara* or *naraba*, if.
Tatoye .. .. *nisiro* or *sitemo*, though.
Nazenareba .. .. *kara*, because.

XI. When the verbs in the infinitive mood are used as nouns, they require the signs of the case; as, *Niti ya watakusi no* suwatte-iru koto *ga yamai no moto de gozarimasu,* My sitting day and night is the cause of my illness.

XII. Relative pronouns are generally omitted in conversation; as, *Sore wa, watakusi ga kosirayemasita hako de gozarimasu,* or *Watakusi ga kosirayemasita hako wa sore de gozarimasu,* That is a box which I have made. Here the relative pronoun *tokorono* ('which' or 'that') ought to be put between the verb *kosiraye-masita* and the object *hako*; but in conversation *tokorono* is not used.

XIII. Adverbs are placed before adjectives and verbs; as, *Sore wa* hanahada *yō gozarimasu,* That is very good; and *Watakusi wa* hayaku *mairimasho,* I shall go quickly.

XIV. When nouns or pronouns are compared with each other, a noun or pronoun which comes directly before the word *yori* or *yorimo* ('than') does not require the sign of case; as, *Anata wa* watakusi yori *takō gozarimasu,* You are taller than I.

XV. After the names of places, *ye* corresponds in English to 'to'; as, *Watakusi wa Yedo* ye *ikimasu,* I go to Yedo. *Ni* corresponds to ' in ' or ' at '; as, *Watakusi wa Asakusa* ni or *Yedo* ni *orimasu,* I live at Asakusa or in Yedo.

XVI. Adjectives for the most part are placed before nouns, but numeral adjectives may be placed after nouns as well as before them; as, *hito san nin* or *san nin no hito,* three persons. When numeral adjectives are applied to persons, *nin* must de added; and when they are placed before nouns, *no* must be put after *nin;* as, *san nin no hito.* There are other words applied to point out the numbers of beasts, birds, trees, &c.

Table.

Hiki, piki, or *biki* is used for quadrupeds:—

Uma { *itt-piki,* one horse.
ni-hiki, two horses.
san-biki, three horses.

Generally, *hiki* is used for all the numbers except 10, 20, 30, up to 100, for which *piki* is used merely for the sake of pronunciation. *Biki* for three, and thousands; as, *zitt piki no uma,* 10 horses; *ni sen biki no uma,* 2000 horses.

Pa, wah, or *ba,* is used for birds:—

Tori { *iti wah,* one bird.
ni wah, two birds.
san ba, three birds.

Wah is used generally; *pa* is for 10, 20, 30, &c.; up to 100, *ba* for 3, and 1000, 2000, &c.

Pon, hon, or *bon* is used for a number of trees or plants:—

Ki { *itt-pon,* one tree.
Ni-hon, two trees.
san bon, three trees.

Hon is of general use; *pon* for 10, 20, 30, &c.; *bon* for 3, and 1000; as, *Watakusi wa konnichi tori san ba,* or (*san ba no tori*) *to san nin no hito,* or *hito san nin, to uma san biki,* or *san biki no uma, to sanbon no ki,* or *ki sanbon, wo mimasita,* I have seen to-day three birds and three persons, and three horses, and three trees.

XVII. *Are* or *arera,* the personal pronouns of the third person, are seldom used; generally the demonstrative adjectives *kono* (this), or *sono* (that), and the nouns *hito* or *okata* (person), are used instead; as, *Watakusi wa kono* okata *wo sakuzitu mimasita,* I have seen him (or this person) yesterday.

XVIII. When any adjective qualifies a noun which is understood, the adjective changes its termination, as follows:—

Adjectives ending *na,* such as *kireina, ōkina,* &c., change their terminations into *ni:*

Kore wa kireina niwa de gozarimasu, It is a beautiful garden.

Kono niwa wa kireini gozarimasu, That garden is a beautiful (one).

Kireina, kireini, beautiful, fine.

Akirakana, akirakani, clear, bright.

Attakana, attakani, warm.

Wazukana, wazukani, or *wazukade,* little, few.
Takusana, takusani, much, many.
Ōkina, ōkini, ōkiwu, large, tall.

Adjectives ending in *ai* or *oi* change their terminations into long *ō*:
Kore wa katai isi de gozarimasu, This is a hard stone.
Kono isi wa katō gozarimasu, This stone is a hard (one).
Katai, katō, hard.
Takai, takō, dear in price, or tall.
Hayai, hayō, quick.
Yowai, yowō, weak.
&c.
Kono ko wa kasikō gozarimasu, This child is a wise (one).
Kasikoi, hasikō, wise, clever.
Tattoi, tattō, precious, worthy.
Tuwoi, tuwō, strong.
Towoi, towō, far.

Those ending in *si* change their terminations into *shu*:
Kono samusa wa kibishu gozarimasu, This winter, or cold, is a severe (one).
Kibisī, kibishu, severe.
Atarasī, atarashu, new.
Tadasī, tadashu, right.
Osorosī, Osoroshu, fearful, horrible.
Otokorasī, otokorashu, manly.
&c.

There are a few exceptions:—Numerical adjectives do not change their terminations, but *de* must be put after them; as, *Watakusi domo wa sannin de gozarimasu,* We are three.

JAPANESE AND ENGLISH EXERCISES.

I.

Watakusi no, my. | *Segare,* son.
Anata no, your. | *Tomodati,* friend.
Kiodai, brother. | *Musume,* daughter, girl.

To, and.

1. *Watakusi no kiodai.* 2. *Anata no tomodati.*
3. *Watakusi no kiodai to anata no tomodati.*

II.

1. My daughter. 2. Your friend. 3. Your son, and my brother.

III.

Kireina*kireini, beautiful. | *Gozarimasu,* is, or are.
Sinsetuna, sinsetuni, kind. |

1. *Sinsetuna tomodati.* 2. *Kireina musume.* 3. *Watakusi no tomodati wa sinsetuni gozarimasu.* 4. *Anata no musume wa kireini gozarimasu.* 5. *Anata no kiodai wa watakusi no tomodati de gozarimasu.*

* See Rule XVIII.

IV.

1. A beautiful girl. 2. Your son is kind. 3. Your daughter is beautiful. 4. My friend is kind. 5. A kind friend.

V.

Watakusi domo no, our. | *Anata gata no,* your.

1. *Watakusi domo no tomodati.* 2. *Anatagata no kiodai.* 3. *Watakusi domo no tomodati wa sinsetuni gozarimasu.* 4. *Anatagata no musume wa kireini gozarimasu.* 5. *Watakusi domo no kiodai wa sinsetuni gozarimasu.*

VI.

1. Our friend. 2. Your daughter. 3. Your daughter is beautiful. 4. Our friend is kind. 5. Your brother is kind.

VII.

Kono, this, these. | *Sono,* that, those.

1. *Kono musume.* 2. *Sono tomodati.* 3. *Sono musume wa kireini gozarimasu.* 4. *Kono tomodati wa sinsetuni gozarimasu.* 5. *Kono segare wa sinsetuni gozarimasu.* 6. *Sono sinsetuna tomodati.* 7. *Kono kireina musume.*

VIII.

1. That son. 2. This friend. 3. This girl is beautiful. 4. That brother is kind. 5. This friend is kind. 6. That beautiful girl. 7. This kind friend.

IX.

Watakusi wa, I. | *Motteimasu,* has, or have.
Anata wa, you. |

1. *Watakusi wa kiodai wo motteimasu.* 2. *Watakusi wa musume wo mottiemasu.* 3. *Anata wa sinsetuna tomodati wo motteimasu.* 4. *Watakusi no tomodati wa kireina musume wo motteimasu.* 5. *Anata no kiodai wa kireina musume wo motteimasu.* 6. *Kono musume wa sinsetuna tomodati wo motteimasu.* 7. *Sono tomodati wa sinsetuna kiodai wo motteimasu.*

X.

1. My brother has a beautiful daughter. 2. Your friend has a kind brother. 3. That girl has a kind brother. 4. I have a beautiful daughter. 5. You have kind brothers. 6. I have kind friends. 7. That beautiful girl has a kind brother.

XI.

Ōkina, ōkiwu, large. | *Tisai, tisana, tisou,**
                        | small, or little.
Shomotu, book.

1. *Watakusi no shomotu wa ōkiwu gozarimasu.* 2. *Anata no shomotu wa tieso gozarimasu.* 3. *Watakusi no kiodai wa ōkina shomotu wo motteimasu.* 4. *Anata no tomodati*

---
* See Rule XVIII.

wa tisana shomotu wo motteimasu. 5. Watakusi no tomodati no shomotu wa ōkiwu gozarimasu. 6. Anata no kiodai wa ōkina shomotu wo motteimasu. 7. Watakusi no tisana segari ga sono ōkina shomotu wo motteimasu. 8. Anata no ōkina kiodai wa sono shomotu wo motteimasu.

XII.

1. My book is small. 2. Your book is large. 3. Your brother has a small book. 4. My friend has a large book. 5. Your father has a small book. 6. My brother's son has that large book. 7. That book is large. 8. This book is small.

XIII.

| Watakusi wa, or ga, motteimasu, I have. | Watakusi ga motteimasu ka? Have I? |
| Anata wa, or ga, motteimasu, you have. | Anata ga motteimasu ka? Have you? |

Ka is always put at the end of an interrogative sentence.

1. Watakusi ga sono shomotu wo motteimasu ka. 2. Anata wa kono shomotu wo motteimasu ka. 3. Anata no tomodati wa shomotu wo motteimasu ka. 4. Watakusi tiesuna segare wa sono ōkina shomotu wo motteimasu ka. 5. Anata no kiodai wasegare wo motteimasu ka. 6. Watakusi no musume wa kono tiesana shomotu wo motteimasu

ka. 7. *Anata wa sono shomotu wo motteimasu ka.*
8. *Watakusi wa sono shomotu wo motteimasu.*

XIV.

1. Have you brothers? 2. I have a brother. 3. Have I that book? 4. Have you that small book? 5. Has your son this book? 6. Has my daughter that book? 7. Have your brothers these large books? 8. My brothers have those small books.

XV.

Watakusi domo wa, or *ga,* we. | *Anatagata wa,* or *ga,* you. *Niwa,* garden.

1. *Watakusi domo wa ōkina niwa wo motteimasu.*
2. *Anatagata wa sono shomotu wo motteimasu ka.* 3. *Watakusi domo wa sono shomotu wo motteimasu.* 4. *Watakusi domo wa sono tiesai shomotu wo motteimasu* 5. *Anatagata wa kiodai wo motteimasu ka.* 6. *Anatagata wa musume wo motteimasu ka.* 7 *Watakusi domo wa tiesai niwa wo motteimasu.* 8. *Anatagata wa niwa wo motteimasu ka.* 9. *Watakusi domo wa niwa wo motteimasu.*

XVI.

1. We have a garden. 2. You have a small garden. 3. Have you brothers? 4. We have brothers. 5. We have daughters. 6. We have large books. 7. You have small books. 8. Have you a son? 9. I have a son.

XVII.

Watakusi domo no, our. | Anatagata no, your.
Motteimasita, had.

1. Watakusi domo no segare ga sono shomotu wo motteimasita. 2. Anatagata no tomodati wa kiodai wo motteimasita. 3. Watakusi wa segare wo motteimasu. 4. Anatagata no musume wa kono shomotu wo motteimasita ka. 5. Watakusi domo no kiodai ga sono ōkina shomotu wo motteimasita. 6. Anatagata no niwa wa ōkiwu gozarimasu ka. 7. Watakusi domo no niwa wa ōkiwu gozarimasu. 8. Anata no niwa wa tiesō gozarimasu.

XVIII.

1. Your garden is large. 2. Your garden is small. 3. Our garden is small. 4. Have your brothers a garden? 5. My brothers have a garden. 6. Have our sons a large book? 7. Our daughter has a small book.

XIX.

Kono
or } okata or hito, this or that person.
Sono

Either of these words is used instead of *are* or *kare*.

* *De* is put after nouns which are placed immediately before *Gozarimasu*.

1. Kono hito ga sono shomotu wo motteimasu. 2. Sono okata wa tiesai shomotu wo motteimasu. 3. Sono hito wa

* See Rule VIII.

Japanese and English Exercises.

watakusi no kiodai de gozarimasu. 4. Kono okata wa anata no tomodati de gozarimasu ka. 5. Sono hito wa watakusi no segare de gozarimasu. 6. Sono hito wa kiodai wo motteimasu. 7. Watakusi no musume wa sono shomotu wo motteimasu. 8. Anata no shomotu wa tiesō gozarimasu.

XX.

1. That person has a book. 2. This person is my brother. 3. Has that person brothers? 4. That person is your friend. 5. Is this person your son? 6. That person is my brother. 7. Have you sons? 8. I have a son. 9. Have you daughters? 10. I have a daughter.

XXI.

Tokei, watch.   Kasa, hat.
Uma, horse.   Hōchō, knife.

Usinaimasita, lost, or has or have lost.
Midasimasita, found, or has or have found.

1. Watakusi wa tokei wo usinaimasita. 2. Anata wa anata no tokei wo midasimasita ka. 3. Watakusi wa hōchō wo usinaimasita. 4. Watakusi no segare wa kasa wo motteimasu. 5. Anatagata no uma wa ōkiwu gozarimasu. 6. Watakusi no musume wa kasa wo usinaimasita. 7. Anatagata wa kasa wo motteimasu ka. 8. Watakusi domo wa uma wo motteimasu. 9. Watakusi no kasa wa ōkiwu gozarimasu. 10. Anata no kaso wa

tiesō gozarimasu ka. 11. *Watakusi no kasa wa ōkiwu gozarimasu.*

XXII.

1. Have you lost your hat? 2. I have lost a hat. 3. Has your son a hat? 4. He (*are wa*) has a hat. 5. Your daughter's hat is large. 6. Our hats are small. 7. We have lost a knife. 8. We have found a watch. 9. Has your brother lost a watch? 10. I have found the watch.

XXIII.

Tegami, letter.
Ye, to.
Ikimasu, go or goes.
Dokoye, where?

† *Uketorimasita*, received, or has or have received.
Mimasita, saw, or has or have seen.

1. *Watakusi wa tegami wo uketorimasita.* 2. *Watakusi wa Yedo ye ikimasu.* 3. *Anata wa Yedo ye ikimasu ka.* 4. *Anata wa tegami wo uketorimasita ka.* 5. *Watakusi no segare ga tegami wo uketorimasita.* 6. *Anatagata wa dokoye ikimasu ka.* 7. *Watakusi domo wa Kanagawa ye ikimasu.* 8. *Watakusi wa anata no kiodai wo mimasita.* 9. *Watakusi no musume wa Asakusa ye ikimasita.* 10. *Anata no kiodai wa tegami wo uketorimasita ka.* 11. *Watakusi no kiodai ga tegami wo uketorimasita.*

XXIV.

1. I have received a letter. 2. You have seen my daughter. 3. I have lost my watch. 4. You go to

Japanese and English Exercises.

Yedo. 5. Where are you going? 6. We are going to Asakusa. 7. My son went (ikimasita) to Kanagawa. 8. We have sons. 9. We went to Yokohama. 10. Your brother went to Yedo. 11. I have beautiful girls. 12. We have found beautiful books. 13. Our daughters are beautiful.

XXV.

Kara, from; *Watakusi no kiodai kara,* from my brother; *Watakusi nō haha kara,* from my mother.

Konniti, to-day.	*Yoi,* good.
Konchō, this morning.	*Warui,* bad.
Sakuzitu, yesterday.	*Mainiti,* every day.

1. *Watakusi wa konniti watakusi no kiodai kara tegami wo uketorimasita.* 2. *Anata wa sakuzitu watakusi no haha kara tegami wo uketorimasita.* 3. *Wakusi domo wa mainiti kono hito wo mimasu.* 4. *Anatagata wa konniti tegaimi wo uketorimasita ka.* 5. *Watakusi domo wa konniti watakusi domo no haha kara tegami wo uketorimasita.* 6. *Anata wa yoi tokei wo motteimasu.* 7. *Watakusi wa konniti tokei wo usinaimasita.* 8. *Watakusi domo no segare ga sono tokei wo midasimasita.* 9. *Sakuzitu watakusi wa kono okata wo mimasita.* 10. *Konniti watakusi wa Yedo ye ikimasu.* 11. *Watakusi domo wa sakuzitu Asakusa ye ikimasita.* 12. *Watakusi wa anata no tomo dati wo konchō mimasita.*

XXVI.

1. I have received a letter from your brother. 2. We have received a letter from our father. 3. Have you received a letter from my brother? 4. We have received a letter from your brother to-day. 5. We are going to Asakusa to-day. 6. We went to Kanagawa yesterday. 7. I have seen your friend this morning. 8. Have you seen your mother to-day? 9. We have lost our watches. 10. We have found your watches. 11. That person has seen your daughter. 12. This person has found your watch. 13. I go to Kanagawa every day.

XXVII.

Ye, to.
Ni, to, for.*

Watakusi no haha ni, to my mother.	*Rondon ye,* to London.
Watakusi no titi ni, to my father.	*Okurimasita,* sent, or has or have sent.
	Okurimasu, send or sends.

1. *Watakusi wa kono tokei wo haha ni okurimasu.* 2. *Anatagata wa sono tokei wo anata no tomodati ni okurimasu ka.* 3. *Watakusi domo wa kono tokei wo watakusi domo no msume ni okurimasu.* 4. *Watakusi wa tegami wo watakusi no haha ni okurimasu.* 5. *Sakuzitu watakusi wa tegami wo watakusi no haha kara uketorimasita.* 6. *Anata wa mainiti tegami wo anata no tomodati ni*

---
* See Note, page 6.

okurimasu ka. 7. *Watakusi wa tegami wo watakusi no haha ni mainiti okurimasu.* 8. *Watakusi no segare ga watakusi ni konniti tegami wo okurimasita.* 9. *Anata wa sakuzitu Asakusa ye ikimasita ka.* 10. *Watakusi wa sakuzitu Kanagawa ye ikimasita.* 11. *Anata wa Kanagawa ye mainiti ikimasu ka.* 12. *Watakusi wa Yokohama ye mainiti ikimasu.*

XXVIII.

1. I have sent a letter to my father. 2. Do you send a letter to your brother every day? 3. We send a letter to our mother every day. 4. Our daughter sent a letter to us (Watakusi domo ye) yesterday. 5. We have received a letter from our friends this morning. 6. Do you receive a letter from your brother every day? 7. I receive a letter from my friends every day. 8. I received a letter from my brother yesterday. 9. We have lost a watch. 10. That person has a good watch. 11. This person has a small (tiesana) watch.

XXIX.

Kore ga, wa, wo, &c., this or these.
Sore ga, wa, &c., that or those.
Oji, uncle.
Tomodati, friend.
Ko, child.

Hito, person.
Wakai, Wakō, young.
Iye, house.
Ki, tree.
Hana, flower.
Binbōna,* *Binboni* or *Binbōde,* poor.

* See Rule XVIII.

1. Watakusi no oji wa wakō gozarimasu. 2. Anata wa kore wo motteimasu ka. 3. Watakusi wa sore wo motteimasu. 4. Watakusi wa ōkina ki wo mimasita. 5. Anata wa sakuzitu kireina hana wo mimasita ka. 6. Watakusi wa konniti sore wo mimasita. 7. Anatagata wa kono hana wo motteimasita ka. 8. Watakusi wa sore wo motteimasita. 9. Kono ko wa tokei wo usinaimasita. 10. Watakusi wa binbōni gozarimasu. 11. Anata wa konniti binbona hito wo mimasita ka.

XXX.

1. I have seen my uncle. 2. Have you seen beautiful flowers? 3. We have seen large trees. 4. That person is poor. 5. My uncle is young. 6. We have lost a watch. 7. We have seen your friends. 8. We went to your house. 9. Have you a garden? 10. We have gardens. 11. I sent a letter to my brother to-day. 12. You received a letter from your father this morning.

XXXI.

Yorimo or yori, more than.

Yorimo ōkiwu, or ōkina,* larger than.	Watakusi no, mine
	Anata no, yours.
Yorimo tisana, or tisō, smaller than.	Watakusi domo no, ours.
	Anatagata no, yours.

Watakusi no niwa wa anata no yori mo ōkiwu gozarimasu, my garden is larger than yours.

* See Rule XVIII.

1. Watakusi no shomotu wa anata no yori mo tiesō gozarimasu. 2. Anata no uma wa watakusi no yori ōkiwu gozarimasu. 3. Anata no shomotu wa watakusi no yorimo yō gozarimasu. 4. Anatagata no uma wa watakusi no yorimo kireini gozarimasu. 5. Anatagata no hōchō wa watakusi domo no yori ōkiwu gozarimasu. 6. Kono hito wa watakusi yorimo binbōni gozarimasu. 7. Kono hana wa sono hana yori kireini gozarimasu. 8. Anata wa kono niwa yori ōkina niwa wo motteimasu ka. 9. Watakusi wa kono niwa yori ōkina no* wo motteimasu. 10. Kono hito wa sono hito yorimo wakō gozarimasu. 11. Kono ki wa sore yorimo ōkiwu gozarimasu. 12. Watakusi no iye wa anata no yorimo tieso gozarimasu. 13. Anata wa kore yorimo tiesana hōchō wo motteimasu ka. 14. Watakusi wa sore yorimo tiesana hōchō wo motteimasu.

XXXII.

1. My house is larger than yours. 2. Your garden is larger than mine. 3. Your flowers are more beautiful than ours. 4. Our house is larger than yours. 5. That person is poorer than this person. 6. Your father is younger than mine. 7. My friend is younger than yours. 8. Our house is smaller than yours. 9. Have you a smaller garden than this? 10. I have a smaller garden than this. 11. Your brother is taller (ōkiwu) than mine. 12. We have a larger house than this.

* Here *no* may be translated into "one."

XXXIII.

Mutukashī, Mutukashū, difficult.
Yasui, Yasuwu, easy, cheap.
Inu, dog.

Neko, cat.
Matti, town or city.
Tuki, moon.
Hosi, star.
Hi, sun.

1. Anata wa neko wo motteimasu ka. 2. Watakusi wa inu wo motteimasu. 3. Anata wa kono shomotu wo mimasita ka. 4. Sono shomotu wa mutukasu gozarimasu. 5. Watakusi no shomotu wa Anata no yorimo yasuwu gozarimasu. 6. Hi wa tuki yorimo ōkiwu gozarimasu. 7. Yedo wa ōkina matti de gozarimasu. 8. Watakusi no tomodati wa Yedo ye ikimasita. 9. Anata wa konniti Asakusa ye ikimasu ka. 10. Watakusi wa konniti yokohama ye ikimasu. 11. Anata no neko wa watakusi no yori ōkiwu gozarimasu. 12. Anata no kiodai wa niwa wo motteimasu ka. 13. Watakusi no titi ga ōkina niwa wo mottcimasu.

XXXIV.

1. My dog is larger than yours. 2. Have you a cat? 3. I have a cat. 4. My house is smaller than yours. 5. Yedo is a large city. 6. The sun is larger than the moon. 7. This book is easier than that. 8. Your book is larger than mine. 9. My book is more difficult than yours. 10. Do you go to Yedo to-day? 11. I go to Yokohama to-day.

XXXV.

Ni, in, or at.
Niwa ni, in the garden.
Uti ni, in the house, or at home.

Orimasu, live, lives, is, are.
Orimasita, lived, was, were.

1. Watakusi wa Yokohama ni orimasu. 2. Anata wa Yokohama ni orimasu ka. 3. Watakusi wa Kanagawa ni orimasu. 4. Watakusi wa Yedo ni orimasita. 5. Konniti watakusi wa uti ni orimasu. 6. Anatagata wa sakuzitu uti ni orimasita. 7. Kireina hana ga niwa ni gozarimasu. 8. Anata no niwa ni kireina hana ga gozarimasu ka. 9. Watakusi no niwa ni ōkina ki ga gozarimasu. 10. Anata wa Asakusa ni orimasita ka. 11. Watakusi wa Yokohama ni orimasita. 12. Anata no niwa ni neko ga orimasu.

XXXVI.

1. Do you live in Yedo? 2. I live in Yokohama. 3. Beautiful flowers are in your garden. 4. Large trees are in my garden. 5. Are (there) beautiful flowers in your garden? 6. Did you live in Yedo? 7. I lived in Kanagawa. 8. Your cat is in my garden. 9. Have you a dog? 10. I have a large dog. 11. Your garden is larger than mine.

XXXVII.

Hana, flower.	Sukimasu, like, likes.
Ringo, apple.	Sukimasita, liked, or has
Nashi, pear.	or have liked.
Itudemo, always.	Watakusi wa hana wo su-
Tabitabi, often.	kimasu, I like flowers.

1. Anata no niwa ni hana ga gozarimasu ka. 2. Watakusi no niwa ni hana ga goza-imasu. 3. Anata wa Asakusa ye tabitabi ikimasu ka. 4. Watakusi wa Yokohama ye tabitabi ikimasu. 5. Anatagata wa ringo wo sukimasu ka. 6. Watakusi domo wa nashi wo sukimasu. 7. Watakusi domo no niwa kireina hana ga gozarimasu. 8. Kono hana wa sono hana yori kireini gozarimasu. 9. Watakusi wa itudemo uti ni orimasu. 10. Anata no tomodati wa tabitabi Yedo ye ikimasu ka. 11. Watakusi no tomodati wa tabitabi Kanagawa ye ikimasu.

XXXVIII.

1. Do you like flowers? 2. I like flowers. 3. Do you go to Yedo often? 4. I go to Yedo often. 5. We like pears. 6. You like apples. 7. Have you flowers? 8. I have an apple. 9. Beautiful flowers are in your garden. 10. I live in Yedo. 11. We often go to Yedo. 12. I have seen beautiful flowers in your garden.

XXXIX.

Iti, one.
Ni, two.
San, three.
Si, four.
Go, five.
Roku, six.
Sitti, seven.
Hatti, eight.
Ku, nine.
Zū, ten.
Zu iti, eleven.
Zu ni, twelve.
Zu san, thirteen.
Zu si, fourteen.
Zu go, fifteen.
Zu roku, sixteen.

Zu siti, seventeen.
Zu hati, eighteen.
Zu ku, nineteen.
Ni zu, twenty.
Ni zu iti, twenty-one.
Ni zu ni, twenty-two.
San˙zu, thirty.
Si zu, forty.
Go zu, fifty.
Roku zu, sixty.
Sitti zu, seventy.
Hatti zu, eighty.
Ku zu, ninety.
H'yaku, hundred.
Sen, thousand.
Man, ten thousand.*

Hitotu, one.
Futatu, two.
Mittu, three.
Yottu, four.
Itutu, five.

Muttu, six.
Nanatu, seven.
Yattu, eight.
Kokonotu, nine.
Tō, ten.†

* This number is used for weight, measure, &c.
† This is for counting ordinary articles, such as chairs, tables, &c.

Shōgatu, January.
Nigatu, February.
Sangatu, March.
Sigatu, April.
Gogatu, May.
Rokugatu, June.

Sitigatu, July.
Hatigatu, August.
Kugatu, September.
Zugatu, October.
Zuittigatu, November.
Zunigatu, December.

Heya, room.
Tukuye, table.
Kosikake, chair.
Nen, year.
Tuki, month.
Takusan, many.
Hikui, or *hikuwu*, low.

Hiroi, or *hirō*, wide.
Kaimasu, buy, or buys.
Kaimasita, bought, or has or have bought.
Wurimasu, sell, sells.
Wurimasita, sold, or has or have sold.

1. Anata wa kiodai wo takusan motteimasu ka. 2. Watakusi wa kiodai wo takusan motteimasu. 3. Anata wa tukuye wo motteimasu ka. 4. Watakusi wa hitotu tukuye wo motteimasu. 5. Anata no niwa ni ki ga futatu gozarimasu. 6. Watakusi no iye ni heya ga mittu gozarimasu. 7. Zu ni tuki ga itti nen di gozarimasu. 8. Anata wa kosikake wo motteimasu ka. 9. Watakusi wa kosikake wo futatu motteimasu. 10. Kono kosikake wa hikuwu gozarimasu. 11. Anata wa sono kosikake wo wurimasu ka. 12. Watakusi wa kono kosikake wo wurimasu. 13. Anata wa kono iye wo kaimasu ka. 14. Watakusi wa kono iye wo kaimasu.

Japanese and English Exercises. 47

XL.

1. Do you sell this chair ? 2. I sell that chair. 3. Do you buy that flower? 4. I buy this table. 5. We have three tables. 6. We have two rooms in (my) house. 7. I sold this flower. 8. Did you live in Yedo? 9. I lived in Yedo three (mi) months. 10. Twelve months make (gozarimasu) one year. 11. We have many chairs. 12. You have many houses. 13. We have three (mittu) houses.

XLI.

Iti, one.	*Siti,* seven.
Ni, two.	*Hati,* eight.
San, three.	*Ku,* nine.
Si, four.	*Zu,* ten.
Go, five.	*Zu iti,* eleven.
Roku, six.	&c.

These are used for measure, weight, hours, or money.

Ni sun, two inches.

Ni, or *san, gō,* two or three *gō,* the *gō* being a measure for liquids and grains.

Ni, or *san toki,* two or three hours.

Ni, or *san bu,* two or three shillings.

Ni means 'by' when it is put before the words 'buy' and 'sell,' as the words *for* or *with* is used in English.

Watakusi wa sono kosikake wa san bu ni kaimasita, or *wurimasita,* I sold or bought that chair *for* three shillings.

Bu, one shilling.
Riyo, four shillings.
Toki, hour.

Gō, a measure for liquids and grain.
Simasu cost, present.
Simasita cost, past.

Ikura, or *ikurani,* how much?

1. *Anata no shomotu wa ikura simasita ka.* 2. *Watakusi no shomotu wa san bu simasita.* 3. *Anata no iye wa ikura simasita ka.* 4. *Watakusi no iye wa h'yaku rigo simasita.* 5. *Anata wa kono tukuye wo ikurani kaimasita ka.* 6. *Watakusi wa kono tukuye wo san riyo ni kaimasita.* 7. *Anata wa kono tukuye wo ikurani wurimasu ka.* 8. *Watakusi wa kono tukuye wo ni riyo ni wurimasu.* 9. *Kono matti* (street) *wa hirō gozarimasu.* 10. *Nizū is toki ga itti nitti* (day) *de gozarimasu.* 11. *Anata wa kono hana wo kaimasu ka.* 12. *Watakusi wa sono ki wo kaimasu.* 13. *Anata wa Yedo ni orimasita ka.* 14. *Watakusi wa Yedo ni iti nen orimasita.*

XLII.

1. How much did your book cost? 2. My book cost three *bu.* 3. How much did you pay for (buy) that table? 4. I bought that table for two *bu.* 5. We sold that chair for two *riyo.* 6. Twenty-four hours are one day. 7. Twelve months are one year. 8. How much does that table cost? 9. That table costs three *riyo.* 10. How much did your house cost (you)? 11. My house cost (me) a hundred *riyo.* 12. I have

a garden. 13. Are there flowers in your garden? 14. In my garden (there) are three trees.

XLIII.

Ni, or *san nin*, for numbers of persons. *Hiki, piki*, or *biki*, for number of quadrupeds; as, *Uma san biki*, three horses; *wa*, or *ba, pa*, for birds.

Tori san ba, or *zit pa*, three or ten birds. *Biki* or *hiki, wa, ba*, or *pa*, are placed after as well as before nouns which they qualify.

Anata no niwa ni tori ga san ba orimasu. There are three birds in your garden.

Niwatori, cock or hen.	*Yamagara*, bullfinch.
Suzume, sparrow.	*Kamo*, wild duck.
Inu, dog.	*Ike*, pond.
Neko, cat.	*Kawa*, river.
Sakana, fish.	

1. *Anata no niwa ni tori ga orimasu ka.* 2. *Watakusi no niwa ni tori ga san ba orimasu.* 3. *Ike ni kamo ga san ba orimasu.* 4. *Anata no iye ni neko ga orimasu ka.* 5. *Watakusi no iye ni neko ga si hiki orimasu.* 6. *Watakusi wa suzume wo go wa mimasita.* 7. *Anatagata wa watakusi no inu wo mimasita ka.* 8. *Watakusi domo wa anato no neko wo mimasita.* 9. *Anata no ike ni kamo ga san ba orimasita.* 10. *Kono kawa ni sakana ga ori-*

masu. 11. *Anata no nina ni yamagara ga si wa orimasu.*
12. *Konchō watakusi wa suzume wo zu ni wa mimasita.*

XLIV.

1. In your garden there are three sparrows. 2. In your pond there is a fish. 3. Have you seen my dog? 4. We have seen your cat. 5. Have you three brothers? 6. I have three daughters. 7. We have three horses. 8. Have you many (*takusan*) houses? 9. We have three houses. 10. My brother has a wild duck. 11. In your garden there are many birds. 12. We have seen three bullfinches this morning. 13. You have seen my garden. 14. In your pond there are three fishes.

XLV.

De means 'in' when it is placed before *aimasu* or *mimasu*, meet, or see. *Watakusi wa kono okata ni matti de aimasita,* I met with this person in the street.

Doko, what place or where?

When 'to see,' or 'meet,' is used, *de* must be put after *doko;* thus, *Doko de anata wa kono hito ni aimasita ka?* Where have you met with him?

When 'to live,' or 'to be,' is used, *ni* must be put after *doko;* thus, *anata wa doko ni orimasu ka,* Where do you live?

Kami, God.
Sekai, world.
Umi, sea, or ocean.
Kosirayemasu, makes, or make.
Kosirayemasita, made, or has or have made.

Oka, land.
Aimasu, meets, or meet.
Aimasita, met, or has or have met.
Konniti, to-day.
Mainiti, every day.

1. *Kami ga sekai wo kosirayemasita.* 2. *Anata wa mainiti kono hito ni aimasu ka.* 3. *Watakusi wa sono hito ni mainiti aimasu.* 4. *Anata wa doko de sono hito ni aimasu ka.* 5. *Watakusi wa kono hito ni Yokohama de aimasu.* 6. *Anatagata wa doko ni orimasu ka.* 7. *Watakusi domo wa Yedo ni orimasu.* 8. *Watakusi no inu wo anata wa doko de mimasita ka.* 9. *Anata no inu wo watakusi wa matti de mimasita.* 10. *Watakusi wa anata no tomodati ni konniti aimasita.* 11. *Watakusi wa tori wo san ba anata no niwa de mimasita.* 12. *Anata no neko ga watakusi no niwa ni orimasu.*

XLVI.

1. Where do you live? 2. I live at Yokohama. 3. Where have you seen that person? 4. I have seen (him) in Yedo. 5. Do you see my friends every day? 6. I see your friends every day. 7. I go to Kanagawa. 8. We met with your brother to-day. 9. Where have you met with my brother? 10. I met with your brother in the street. 11. God created the world. 12. In your garden I saw two cats.

XLVII.

Itu, when, used interrogatively.
Nan doki ni, at what time or hour?
Nan riyo, how many riyo?
Nan ri,* how many miles?
Nan nin, how many persons?

Kane, money or metal.
Koko, here.
Made, into.
Kara, from.
Suguto, immediately.
Zinmin, people.
Niti-niti, every day.
Minato, seaport.

1. Koko kara minato made nan ri gozarimasu ka. 2. San ri gozarimasu. 3. Anata wa Yokohama ye itu ikimasu ka. 4. Watakusi wa Yokohama ye konniti ikimasu. 5. Anata wa kono iye wo kaimasita ka. 6. Watakusi wa kono iye wo kaimasita. 7. Anata no iye wa nan riyo simasita ka. 8. Watakusi no iye wa h'yaku riyo simasita. 9. Anata wa nan doki ni Yokohama ye ikimasu ka. 10. Watakusi wa Yokohama ye zu ni zi ni (12 o'clock) ikimasu. 11. Anata no iye ni hito ga nan nin orimasu ka. 12. Watakusi no iye ni hito ga roku nin orimasu. 13. Ikura anata wa kane wo motteimasu ka. 14. Watakusi wa kane wo zu riyo motteimasu.

XLVIII

1. How much money have you? 2. I have three riyo. 3. At what time do you go to Yedo? I go to

---

* After the words *nan ri*, the sign of case is not put.

Yedo at 12 o'clock. 5. How many miles are there from here to Kanagawa ? 6. (There) are three miles from here to Kanagawa. 7. How many persons are there in your house ? 8. There are ten persons in my house. 9. When are you going to your friend's house ? 10. I go to my friend's house to-day. 11. I go to my house immediately.

XLIX.

Takusan, much, or many. *Watakusi wa saké wo takusan nomimasita,* I have drunk much rice-spirits.

Watakusi wa takusan shomotu wo motteimasu, I have many books.

Wazuka, a little or few.

Watakusi wa wazuka kane wo motteimasu, I have a little money.

Watakusi wa wazuka shomotu wo motteimasu, I have a few books.

Pan, bread.
Niku, meat.
Saké, rice-spirit.
Midu, water.
Tabemasu, eats, or eat.

Nomimasu, drinks, or drink.
Tabemasita, ate, or has or have eaten.
Nomimasita, drank, or has or have drunk.

1. *Kono okata wa niku wo tabemasu ka.* 2. *Kono okata wa pan wo tobemasu.* 3. *Anata wa niku wo takusan motteimasu ka.* 4. *Watakusi wa wazuka niku wo motteimasu.* 5. *Anata no tomodati wa saké wo nomimasu ka.* 6. *Watakusi no tomodati wa midu wo nomimasu.* 7. *Watakusi*

domo wa niku wo takusan tabemasita. 8. *Watakusi no kiodai wa sake wo wazuka nomimasu.* 9. *Anata wa kane wo takusan mottemasu ka.* 10. *Watakusi wa wazuka kane wo motteimasu.* 11. *Ikura anata wa kane wo motteimasu ka.* 12. *Watakusi wa kane wo san riyo motteimasu.* 13. *Anata no niwa ni takusan hana ga gozarimasu ka.* 14. *Watakusi no niwa ni wazuka hana ga gozarimasu.*

L.

1. Have you many books? 2. I have a few books. 3. Are there many trees in your garden? 4. There are a few trees in my garden. 5. We have much rice-spirit. 6. Do you eat meat? 7. I eat bread. 8. Do you drink water? 9. I drink rice-spirit. 10. I have drunk a little rice-spirit. 11. We have eaten much meat. 12. You have drunk much water. 13. We have many houses. 14. You have many friends.

LI.

ァ *Amari,* too.

Anata wa amari takusan kane wo motteimasu. You have too much money.

To, ... *to,* and.

Watakusi to anata to ga ikimasu. I and you go.

Watakusi wa konniti inu to neko to wo mimasita.* I have seen a dog and cat to-day.

*.See Rule III.

Satō, sugar.
Konniti, to-day.
Sumi, ink.
Kurō, 'kuroi, black.
Sukimasu, like, or likes.

Kiraimasu, dislike, or dislikes.
Hiru maye, before noon.
Urimasita, sold, or has or have sold.

1. Anata wa satō wo sukimasu ka. 2. Watakusi wa satō wo kiraimasu. 3. Kono sumi wa amari kurō gozarimasu. 4. Konniti hirumaye ni watakusi domo wa Yedo ye ikimasu. 5. Anata wa itu Yokohama ye ikimasu ha. 6. Watakusi wa Yokohama ye konniti ikimasu. 7. Watakusi wa watakusi no kiodai to anata no tomodati wo mimasita. 8. Niti-niti watakusi wa anata no kiodai to tomodati wo mimasu. 9. Watakusi wa saké to midu wo sukimasu. 10. Anata no iye wa ikura simasita ka. 11. Watakusi no iye wa h'yaku riyo simasita. 12. Anata wa anata no neko wo urimasita ka. 13. Watakusi wa watakusi no inu wa urimasita.

LII.

1. You have too much money. 2. You and I go to Yokohama. 3. We have too many trees in our garden, or, There are too many trees in our garden. 4. I saw my brother and your friend. 5. When are you going to Yokohama? 6. We are going to Yokohama to-day. 7. Do you see your friend every day? 8. I see my friend every day. 9. My mother and father go to Yedo to-day. 10. How much did your brother's house cost?

11. Your brother's house cost 200 *riyo*. 12. You have too many horses. 13. We saw a cat and dog in your garden to day.

LIII.

Dare ga, no, or *wo,* who, whose, or whom? in the interrogative sense.

Dare ga kimasita ka, who came (here)?
Dare wo anata wa mimasita ka, whom have you seen?
Nani ga, wo, or *no,* what?
Anata wa nani wo mimasita ka, what have you seen?
Anata no niwa ni nani ga orimasu ka, what is there in your garden?

׀	*Hako,* box.	*Cha,* tea.
׀	*Kutu,* boot, or shoe.	*Tebukuro,* glove.
	Sekihitu, pencil.	

1. *Dare ga watakusi no hako wo motteimasu ka.* 2. *Anata no tomodati ga anata no hako wo motteimasu.* 3. *Anata wa dare wo mimasita ka.* 4. *Watakusi wa anata no kiodai wo mimasita.* 5. *Anata no niwa ni nani ga orimasu ka.* 6. *Watakusi no niwa ni tori ga orimasu.* 7. *Anata wa nani wo motteimasu ka.* 8. *Watakusi wa kane wo motteimasu.* 9. *Anata wa konniti nani wo mimasita ka.* 10. *Konniti watakusi wa uma wo mimasita.* 11. *Anata wa dare no shomotu wo motteimasu ka.*

Japanese and English Exercises.

12. *Watakusi no tomodati no shomotu wo motteimasu.*
13. *Anata wa nani wo sukimasu ka.* 14. *Watakusi wa cha wo sukimasu.* 15. *Anata no tebukuro wa ikura simasita ka.* 16. *Watakusi no tebukuro wa san bu simasita.*

LIV.

1. What have you? 2. I have gloves. 3. Whom have you seen? 4. I have seen your brother. 5. Who has my books? 6. My friend has your books. 7. What have you seen in (*de*) my garden? 8. I have seen a cat in your garden. 9. Do you drink tea? 10. I drink water. 11. Do you like sugar? 12. I like sugar. 13. Whose book have you? 14. I have my book. 15. How much did your pencil cost? 16. My pencil cost (H'yaku mon) a penny.

LV.

Ōkina,
Ōkiwu, } large, or great.   *Yorimo,*
or Yori, } *ōkiwu,* or *ōkina,* larger, or greater.

Itiban { *ōkiwu,*
ōkina, } largest, or greatest.

Yoi,
Yō, } good.   *Yori* { *yoi,*
yō, } better.*   *Ittiban* { *yoi,*
yō, } best.

* See Rule XVIII.

58   Japanese and English Exercises.

Chonin, merchant.
Yama, mountain.
Tori, bird.

Tiesai, tiesō, small.
Jobu, jobuni, strong.

1. Watakusi no iye wa anata no (yours) yori ōkiwu gozarimasu. 2. Anata no niwa wa watakusi no yori tiesō gozarimasu. 3. Kono tori wa sono tori yori ōkiwu gozarimasu. 4. Anata wa kore (that) yori ōkina iye wo motteimasu ka. 5. Kono iye ga watakusi no ittiban ōkina iye de gozarimasu. 6. Watakusi no iye wa jobuni gozarimasu. 7. Anata no niwa wa watakusi no yori yō gozarimasu. 8. Anata no shomotu ga ittiban yō gozarimasu. 9. Anata no niwa ni tori ga orimasu ka. 10. Tori wa yama ni takusan orimasu. 11. Anata wa chonin de gozarimasu ka. 12. Watakusi wa chonin de gozarimasu. 13. Anata wa kore yori ōkina kutu wo motteimasu ka. 14. Kore ga ittiban ōkina kutu de gozarimasu.

LVI.

1. Your book is better than mine. 2. Have you a larger house than this? 3. This is my largest house. 4. My house is smaller than yours. 5 Have you larger boots than these? 6. These are my largest boots. 7. Are there many birds in the mountains? 8. There are many birds in the mountains. 9. Are you a merchant. 10. I am a merchant.

Japanese and English Exercises.

LVII.

Dare kara, from whom? | *Dare ni,* or *ye,* to whom?
Dare no de, whose one?

Itiban, first.	*Rokuban,* sixth.
Niban, second.	*Sitiban,* seventh.
Sanban, third.	*Hattiban,* eighth.
Siban, fourth.	*Kuban,* ninth.
Goban, fifth.	*Zuban,* tenth.

Nitiyoniti, Sunday.	*Mokuyoniti,* Thursday.
Getuyoniti, Monday.	*Kinyoniti,* Friday.
K'wayoniti, Tuesday.	*Doyoniti,* Saturday.
Suiyoniti, Wednesday.	

Kerai, servant.
Gejo, maidservant.
Kokoni, here.
Konniti, to-day, or this [day.
Sokoni, there.
Orimasu, lives, or live.

Orimasita, lived, or has or have lived.
Uketorimasu, receives, or receive.
Uketorimasita, received, or has or have received.

1. *Kono shomotu wa dare no de gozarimasu ka.* 2. *Sono shomotu wa watakusi no de gozarimasu.* 3. *Konniti dare kara tegami wo uketorimasita ka.* 4. *Konniti watakusi wa tegami wo watakusi no tomodati kara uketorimasita.* 5. *Konniti wa nitiyoniti de gozarimasu ka.* 6. *Konniti wa getuyoniti de gozarimasu.* 7. *Anata no kerai wa kokoni oriwasu.* 8. *Anata no gejo wa sokoni orimasu.* 9. *Kono tegami wo anata wa dare ye okurimasu ka* (send).

10. *Watakusi wa kono tegami wo kiodai ye okurimasu.*
11. *Anata wa sono tegami wa anata no tomodati ye okurimasu ka.* 12. *Watakusi wa kore wo watakusi no haha ni okurimasu.*

LVIII.

1. To whom do you send this letter? 2. I send that to my friend. 3. Where is my servant? 4. Your servant is here. 5. Is my maidservant there? 6. Here is your maidservant. 7. From whom have you received that letter? 8. I have received this letter from my brother. 9. Whose is this book? 10. That is mine. 11. Is this day Monday? 12. This day is Tuesday.

LIX.

Indicative Mood. Present.
Motteiru, to have.

Watakusi ga, or *wa motteimasu,*	I have.
Anata ga, or *wa motteimasu* .	you have.
Kono ⎫ or ⎬ *hito* or *okata*	she or he had.
Sono ⎭	
Watakusi domo	we have.
Anatagata	you have.
*Kono ⎫ or ⎬ *hito,* or *okata* . .	they have.
Sono ⎭	

* As we have the same form of the verb in all persons, singular or plural, we do not repeat them all here.

Japanese and English Exercises. 61

Kane, money.
K~~asa,~~ hat.
Heya, room.

Tanmono, cloth.
Haori, coat.
Kushi, comb.

1. *Anata wa kane wo motteimasu ka.* 2. *Watakusi wa kane wo takusan motteimasu.* 3. *Anatagata wa kasa wo motteimasu ka.* 4. *Watakusi domo wa kasa wo motteimasu.* 5. *Kono okata wa heya wo motteimasu ka.* 6. *Kono okata wa heya wo motteimasu.* 7. *Anata no tomodati wa ōkina niwa wo motteimasu ka.* 8. *Watakusi no tomodati wa ōkina iye wo motteimasu.* 9. *Anata no kiodai wa tanmono wo motteimasu ka.* 10. *Watakusi no tomodati wa haori wo motteimasu.*

LX.

1. Have you a comb? 2. I have a comb. 3. Have you hats? 4. We have hats. 5. He has a coat. 6. Has she cloth? 7. She has cloth. 8. Has your brother a room. 9. My brother has a room. 10. Have your friends much money? 11. My brothers have much money.

LXI.

Indicative Mood. Past.

Watakusi ga, or wa motteimasita . . I had.
Anata ga . . . . . . you had.
Kono ⎫
 or ⎬ okata . . . . . he had.
Sono ⎭

Watakusi domo wa motteimasita . . we had.
Anatagata . . . . . . you had.
Kono
 or } *okata* . . . . . he had.
Sono

Izen, formerly. | *Imani,* presently.
Ima, now, this time. | *Suguto,* directly.

1. *Anata wa kono shomotu wo ina motteimasu ka.*
2. *Watakusi wa kono shomotu wo izen motteimasita.*
3. *Anatagata wa heya wo motteimasu ka.* 4. *Watakusi domo wa heya wo motteimasu.* 5. *Anata wa kane wo motteimasita ka.* 6. *Watakusi wa kane wo motteimasita.* 7. *Anata no tomodati wa iye wo motteimasu ka.* 8. *Watakusi no tomodati wa izenniye wo motteimasita.* 9. *Watakusi no kiodai wa takusan kane wo motteimasu ka.* 10. *Sono chonin wo tanmono wo motteimasita.* 11. *Kono chōnin wa tanmono wo motteimasu.*

LXII.

1. Had you a house? 2. We had a house. 3. Had you this book? 4. I had that book formerly. 5. We had a horse. 6. Had your brother a room. 7. My brother had a room. 8. Have you many friends now? 9. I had many friends. 10. We had many books.

Japanese and English Exercises. 63

LXIII.

Indicative Mood. Present, negatively.

Masen, have not, or has not.

Watakusi wa or *ga motteimasen*	I have not.
Anata wa	you have not.
Kono ⎫ or ⎬ *okata wa* . . . . *Sono* ⎭	she or he has not.
Watakusi domo wa . .	we have not.
Anata gata wa . . .	you have not.
Kono ⎫ or ⎬ *okata wa* . . . *Sono* ⎭	they have not.

Toki ni or *niwa,* when, or at the time.	*Orimasu,* live.
	Orimasita, lived.
Kara, because.	*Sakuzitu,* yesterday.
Nipon, Japan.	*Ye,* to.
Ni, in, or at. [speaks.	*Kotoba,* word, or lan-
Hanasimasu, speak or	guage.

Anata wa Nipon ni orimasita tokini, (*anata wa) *takusan kane wo motteimasita ka,* or *Nipon ni orimasita tokini, anata wa takusan kane wo motteimasita ka.* Had you much money when you were in Japan?

Nipon ni orimasita kara, wutakusi wa Nipon kotoba wo hanasimasu. I speak Japanese because I lived in Japan.

1. *Anata wa kane wo motteimasu ka.* 2. *Watakusi wa kane wo motteimasen.* 3. *Anatagata wa heya wo motteimasu ka.* 4. *Watakusi domo wa heya wo motteimasen.*

* Here *anata wa* (you) is generally understood.

64   *Japanese and English Exercises.*

5. *Anata wa takusan tomodati wo motteimasu ka.* 6. *Watakusi wa takusan tomodati wo motteimasen.* 7. *Anata no tomodati wa uma wo motteimasu ka.* 8. *Watakusi no tomodati wa uma wo motteimasen.* 9. *Nipon ni orimasita tokini anata wa kane wo takusan motteimasita ka.* 10. *Watakusi wa, Nipon ni orimasita tokini, takusan kane wo motteimasita.* 11. *Watakusi wa Nipon ni orimasita kara, Nipon kotoba wo hanasimasu.* 12. *Anata wa izen Yokohama ni orimasita ka.* 13. *Watakusi wa izen Yedo ni orimasita.* 14. *Ima anata wa doko ni orimasu ka.* 15. *Ima watakusi wa Yokohama ni orimasu.*

LXIV.

1. Have you much money? 2. I had much money when I was in Japan. 3. Have you a horse? 4. I have no (have not) horse. 5. Had you many houses when you were in England (Igilisu). 6. We had three houses when we were in England. 7. Has your brother a room? 8. He has no room. 9. Did you live in Yedo formerly? 10. I lived formerly in Yokohama. 11. Where do you live now? 12. I live in Yedo now.

LXV.

Indicatve Mood. Past tense, negatively.

Watakusi wa motteimasenanda   I had not.
Anata wa   .   .   .   .   you had not.
Kono
 or } *okata*   .   .   .   she or he had not.
Sono

Japanese and English Exercises.

Watakusi domo wa motteimasenanda, we had not.
Anata gata . . . . you had not.
Kono
or } okata . . . . she or he had not.
Sono

Mi tuki izen ni, three months ago.
Roku nen izen ni, six years ago.

Kimasita, came, or has or have come.	Kaimasu, buy, or buys.
Ikutu, how old, how many	Haori, coat.
Ikura, how much.	Kimono, dress.

1. Anata wa mi tuki izen ni Nipon ye kimasita ka.
2. Watakusi wa itti nen izen ni Nipon ye kimasita.
3. Anata no kiodai wa ikutu de gozarimasu ka. 4. Watakusi no kiodai wa zu ni de gozarimasu. 5. Kono okata wa Yokohama kara kimasita ka. 6. Sono okata wa Yedo kara kimasita. 7. Anata wa Yokohama ni orimasita tokiniwa, takusan tomodati wo motteimasenanda ka. 8. Watakusi wa Yokohama ni orimasita tokiniwa tomodati wo motteimasenanda. 9. Kono haori wa ikura simasita ka. 10. Kono haori wa san riyo simasita. 11. Anata wa sono kimono wo kaimasu ka. 12. Watakusi wa sono kimono wo kaimasen.

LXVI.

1. When you were in Japan, had you many friends?
2. When I was in Japan, I had many friends. 3. How

much does this coat cost? 4. This coat cost three riyo. 5. We have many houses in Yedo. 6. Did you come to Japan three days (mittka izen) ago? 7. I came to Japan three months ago. 8. How old are you? 9. I am twelve (years old). 10. Do you buy this dress? 11. I do not buy this dress.

LXVII.

Indicative Mood. Future.

Watakusi wa or *ga motteimasho*	I shall have.
Anata	you will have.
Kono okata	she or he will have
Watakusi domo . . .	we shall have.
Anata gata	you will have.
Kono okata	they will have.

Miyo niti, to-morrow.
Miyo ban, to-morrow evening.
Miyo asa, to-morrow morning.

Ikimasho, will or shall go.
Uketorimasho, will or shall receive.
Mimasho, will or shall see.

1. *Watakusi ga sono hako wo motteimasho* (shall hold). 2. *Anata no tomodati wa Asakusa ye miyo niti ikimasu ka.* 3. *Watakusi no tomodati wa miyo asa Asakusa ye ikimasho.* 4. *Watakusi wa sono shomotu wo miyo ban mimasho.* 5. *Itu anata no tomodati ga kono tegami wo*

uketorimasho ka. 6 Watakusi no tomodati ga sono tegami wo miyo ban uketorimasho. 7. Watakusi domo wa miyo niti Anala no iye wo mimasho. 8. Watakusi wa sono kane wo miyo niti uketorimasho. 9. Itu kono okata wa Yedo ye ikimasho ka. 10. Sono okata wa Yedo ye miyo niti ikimasho. 11. Itu anata wa kono tegami wo uketorimasita ka. 12. Watakusi wa kono tegami wo sakuzitu uketorimasita.

LXVIII.

1. When will you go to Yedo? 2. I shall go to Yedo to-morrow. 3. Shall I hold this box? 4. I shall hold that book. 5. When do you receive your money? 6. I shall receive my money to-morrow morning. 7. You will go to Asakusa to-morrow evening. 8. Shall we see that book to-day? 9. We shall see this book to-morrow. 10. When have you seen (did you see) my friend? 11. I have seen (saw) your friend yesterday.

LXIX.

Indicative Mood. Future, negatively.

Watakusi wa motteimasumai .	I shall not have.
Anata wa motteimasumai .	you will not have.
Kono okata wa . . .	he will not have.
Watakusi domo . . .	we shall not have.
Anata gata	you will not have.
Kono okata	they will not have.

F 2

Ikimasumai, shall or will not go.
Mimasumai, shall or will not see.
Kimusumai, shall or will not come.
Made, till.

1. *Anata no tomodati wa konniti Yedo ye ikimasu ka.*
2. *Watakusi no tomodati wa konniti Yedo ye ikimasen.*
3. *Anata wa miyo niti Asakusa ye ikimasho ka.* 4. *Watakusi wa miyo niti Asakusa ye ikimasumai.* 5. *Anata no kiodai wa miyo ban Kanagawa ye ikimasho ka.* 6. *Watakusi no kiodai wa miyo ban Kanagawa ye ikimasumai.* 7. *Anata no tomodati wa miyo niti anata no iye ni kimasho ka.* 8. *Watakusi no tomodati wa niyo niti watakusi no iye ni kimasumai.* 9. *Kono hito wa sono kane wo miyo ban made motteimasho ka* (will keep)? 10. *Sono hito wa kono kane wo miyo ban made motteimasumai.* 11. *Anata wa kono okata wo miyo niti mimasho ka.* 12. *Watakusi wa kono hito wo miyo niti mimasumai.*

LXX.

1. I shall not go to Yedo to-morrow. 2. Shall we go to Yokohama? 3. We shall not go to Yokohoma to-morrow. 4. Will your friends come to my house? 5. My friends will not come to your house. 6. You will see my friend to-day. 7. I shall not see your brother to-morrow, because I shall go to Yedo. 8. Where will you go to-morrow? 9. I shall go to Kanagawa to-morrow. 10. I shall wait (matteimasho)

Japanese and English Exercises.

till you come. 11. How much did this coat cost? 12. This coat cost three riyo.

LXXI.

Iku, to go.
Kiku, to hear.
Suku, to like.

Hasiru, to run.
Sosiru, to sneer at.

Indicative. Present.

Ikimasu, go, or goes.
Kikimasu, hear, or hears.
Sukimasu, like, or likes.
Ikimasen, do not go, or does not go.
Kikimasen, do not hear, or does not hear.
Sukimasen, do not like, or does not like.

1. *Nani wo anata wa sukimasu ka.* 2. *Watakusi wa saké wo sukimasu.* 3. *Konniti anata wa dokoye ikimasu ka.* 4. *Watakusi wa konniti Yedo ye ikimasu.* 5. *Anata no tomodati wa sono shomotu wo sukimasen ka.* 6. *Watakusi no tomodati wa sono shomotu wo sukimasen.* 7. *Anata wa konniti Asakusa ye ikimasen ka.* 8. *Watakusi wa konniti ikimasen.* 9. *Anata no kiodai wa hana wo sukimasu ka.* 10. *Watakusi no kiodai wa hana wo sukimasen.* 11. *Anata no musume wa konniti Kanagawa ye ikimasu ka.* 12. *Watakusi no musume wa konniti Kanagawa ye ikimasen.*

LXXII.

1. Do you like flowers? 2. I do not like flowers. 3. Where do you go? 4. I go to Yedo. 5. When do you go to Asakusa? 6. I go to Asakusa to-day. 7. Does your brother like saké? 8. My brother does not like saké. 9. Does your son like meat (niku)? 10. My son likes meat. 11. Where does your friend go? 12. My friend goes to his room (heya).

LXXIII.

Indicative. Past.

Sukimasita, liked, or has or have liked.
Ikimasita, went, or has or have gone.
Kikimasita, heard, or has or have heard.
Hasirimasita, ran, or has or have run.
Sosirimasita, sneered at, or has or have sneered at.

Negatively.

Sukimasenanda, has or have not liked.
Ikimasenanda, has or have not gone.
Kikimasenanda, has or have not heard.
Hasirimasenanda, has or have not run.
Sosirimasenanda, has or have not sneered.

| *Hanasi,* story. | *Hayaku,* quickly. |
| *Sinbun,* news. | *Hito,* person, or others. |

1. *Sakuzitu anata wa Yedo ye ikimasita ka.* 2. *Wata-*

kusi wa sakuzitu Yedo ye ikimasenanda. 3. *Doko ye anata no kiodai wa ikimasita ka.* 4. *Watakusi no kiodai wa Kanagawa ye ikimasita.* 5. *Itu anata wa sono sinbun wo kikimasita ka.* 6. *Watakusi wa sono sinbun wo sakuzitu kikimasita.* 7. *Anata wa kono hanasi wo kikimasita ka.* 8. *Watakusi wa sono hanasi wo kikimasenanda.* 9. *Anata no segare wa hayaku hasirimasu ka.* 10. *Watakusi no segare wa hayaku hasirimasen.* 11. *Anata wa izen kono hana wo sukimasita ka.* 12. *Watakusi wa izen sono hana wo sukimasita.*

LXXIV.

1. Did you like my house? 2. I liked your house. 3. Did you hear that news? 4. I heard that news yesterday. 5. Did you run quickly? 6. I did not run quickly. 7. Does my friend sneer at others? 8. Your friend sneered at others yesterday. 9. Did you go to your brother's house? 10. I went to my brother's house.

LXXV.

Indicative Mood. Future.

Sukimasho, will or shall like.
Ikimasho, will or shall go.
Kikimasho, will or shall hear.
Hasirimasho, will or shall run.
Sosirimasho, will or shall sneer at.

Sukimasumai, will or shall not like.
Ikimasumai, will or shall not go.
Kikimasumai, will or shall not hear.

1. *Anata no kiodai wa sono shomotu wo sukimasho ka.*
2. *Watakusi no kiodai wa sono shomotu wo sukimasho.*
3. *Anata wa miyo niti Yedo ye ikimasho ka.* 4. *Watakusi wa miyo niti Yedo ye ikimasumai.* 5. *Watakusi domo wa sono hanasi wo miyo niti kikimasho.* 6. *Anata no musume wa kono hana wo sukimasho ka.* 7. *Watakusi no musume wa sono hana wo sukimasumai.* 8. *Anata wa doko ye ikimasu ka.* 9. *Watakusi Kanagawa ye ikimasu.* 10. *Itu anata no tomodati wa Asakusa ye ikimasita ka.* 11. *Watakusi no tomodati wa sakuzitu Asakusa ye ikimasita.* 12. *Watakusi no kiodai wa miyo niti Yedo ye ikimasumai.*

LXXVI.

1. Will you go to Yedo to-morrow? 2. I shall not go to Yedo to-morrow. 3. Where will your brother go? 4. My brother will go to Asakusa. 5. Will your daughter like that flower? 6. My daughter will not like that flower. 7. We shall hear that story to-morrow evening. 8. Does your brother run quickly? 9. My brother runs quickly. 10. Where did your friend go? 11. My friend went to Kanagawa.

LXXVII.

Tokeru, to melt.
Kangayeru, to think.
Taduneru, to seek.
Okiru, to get up.
Miru, to see.
Otiru, to fall.

Indicative. Present.

Tokemasu, melt or melts.
Kangayemasu, think or thinks.
Tadunemasu, look for or looks for.
Okimasu, get up or gets up.
Mimasu, see or sees.
Otimasu, fall or falls.
Tokemasen, has or have not melted.
Kangayemasen, has or have not thought.

Ame, rain.
Yuki, snow.
Maiasa, every morning.
Mainiti, every day.
Attakani, warm.
Iti zi, one o'clock.
Ni zi, two o'clock.
Hati zi, eight o'clock.
Tenki, weather.

1. Nan doki ni anata wa maiasa okimasu ka. 2. Watakusi wa maiasa hatti zi ni okimasu. 3. Nani wo anata wa mainiti mimasu ka. 4. Watakusi wa mainiti shomotu wo mimasu. 5. Tenki ga attakani gozarimasu kara yuki ga tokemasu. 6. Anata no tomodati wa mainiti anata no kiodai wo mimasu. 7. Konniti wa attakani gozarimasu kara yuki ga tokemasu. 8. Anata wa nani wo kangayemasu ka. 9. Watakusi wa shomotu wo kongayemasu. 10. Anata no musume wa nani wo tadunemasu ka.

11. *Watakusi no musume wa shomotu wo tadunemasu.*
12. *Anata no tomodati wa mainiti nan doki ni okimasu ka.* 13. *Watakusi no tomodati wa maiasa hati zi ni okimasu.* 14. *Yuki ga tokemasen.* 15. *Watakusi wa konniti tomodati wo mimasen.*

LXXVIII.

1. At what time do your friends get up? 2. They get up at eight o'clock. 3. What does your brother look for? 4. My brother looks for (his) books. 5. What do you think of? 6. Do you see your friends every day? 7. I see my friends every morning. 8. I think about (my) books. 9. Do you get up every morning at eight? 10. I get up at eight every morning. 11. Do your daughters see books? 12. My daughters see books. 13. I do not see your friends. 14. I do not look for books.

LXXIX.

Indicative Mood. Past.

Tokemasita, melt, or has or have melted.
Kangayemasita, thought, or has or have thought.
Tadunemasita, looked for, or has or have looked for.
Okimasita, got up, or has or have got up.
Mimasita, saw, or has or have seen.
Okimasita, fell, or has or have fallen.
Tokemasenanda, has or have not melted.
Kangayemasenanda, has or have not thought.
Tadunemasenanda, has or have not looked for.

Japanese and English Exercises.

Konchō, this morning.
Naze, why.
Koto, matter.
Dōsite, how.
Kimono, dress.

1. *Yuki ga konchō tokemasita.* 2. *Anata wa konchō nan doki ni okimasita ka.* 3. *Watakusi wa konchō hatti zi ni okimasita.* 4. *Konniti wa attakani gozarimasen kara yuki ga takemasen.* 5. *Anata wa kono koto wo kangayemasita ka.* 6. *Watakusi wa sono koto wo kongayemasenanda.* 7. *Anata wa sakuzitu nani wo Asakusa de mimasita ka.* 8. *Watakusi wa sakuzitu Asakusa de tori wo mimasita.* 9. *Anata wa nani wo tadunemasu ka.* 10. *Watakusi wa kimono wo tadunemasu.* 11. *Anata wa naze kono shomotu wo sukimasen ka.* 12. *Sono shomotu wa omosiroku* (amusing) *gozarimasen kara watakusi wa sukimasen.* 13. *Anata wa konniti watakusi no segare wo mimasita ka.* 14. *Watakusi wa anata no tomodati wo mimasita.*

LXXX.

1. Have you thought about that matter? 2. I did not think about that matter. 3. What are you looking for? 4. I look for your brother's book. 5. What time did you get up this morning? 6. I got up this morning at eight o'clock. 7. Why have you not seen my friend yesterday? 8. I have not seen your friend yesterday, because I did not go to Yokohama. 9. Where did you go yesterday? 10. I went to Asakusa yester-

day. 11. What does your brother look for? 12. My brother looks for (his) book.

LXXXI.
Indicative Mood. Future.

Tokemasho, will or shall melt.
Kangayemasho, will or shall think.
Tadunemasho, will or shall look for.
Okimasho, will or shall get up.
Mimasho, will or shall see.
Tokemasumai, will or shall not melt.
Kangayemasumai, will or shall not think.
Okimasumai, will or shall not get up.

Miyo niti, to-morrow. | *Hayaku*, early.
Miyo asa, to-morrow morning.

1. *Miyo niti yuki ga tokemasho ka.* 2. *Miyo niti yuki wa tokemasumai.* 3. *Anata no tomodati wa miyo asa nan doki ni okimasho ka.* 4. *Watakusi no tomodati wa miyo niti hatti zi ni okimasho ka.* 5. *Anata wa miyo asa hayaku okimasho ka.* 6. *Watakusi wa miyo asa hayaku okimasumai.* 7. *Anata wa nani wo usinaimasita ka.* 8. *Watakusi wa kane wo usinaimasita.* 9. *Anata wa sore wo tadunemasita ka.* 10. *Watakusi wa sore wo tadunemasenanda.* 11. *Anata no kiodai wa miyo niti watakusi no tomodati wo nimasho ka.* 12. *Watakusi no kiodai wa miyo niti Yedo ye ikimasen kara, Anata no*

Japanese and English Exercises. 77

tomodati wo mimasumai. 13. *Naze anata no kiodai wa miyo niti Yedo ye ikimasumai ka.* 14. *Watakusi no kiodai wa biyokide* (ill) *gozarimasu kara ikimasumai.*

LXXXII.

1. What time will you get up to-morrow morning? 2. I shall get up to-morrow morning at eight o'clock. 3. Will you see me to-morrow in Yedo? 4. I shall not see you to-morrow. 5. Does your daughter get up early every morning? 6. She gets up every morning at six o'clock (*roku zi*). 7. Why do your friends go to Yedo to-day? 8. My friends go to Yedo because (they) have (their) houses (there). 9. What do you look for? 10. I look for my books. 11. Have you lost (your) money? 12. I have lost my knife (*hōchō*).

LXXXIII.

Indicative. Present.

Kuru, to come.
Suru, to do.
Kioiku sure, to educate.

Zonzuru, to know.
Kurū, to be wild.
Kanzuru, to admire.

Kimasu, come or comes.
Simasu, do or does.
Kioiku simasu, educate or educates.
Kanzimasu, admire or admires.

Ki, mind.
Zinmin, people.
Dō or *Dosite*, how.

Saiku, workmanship.
Ye, picture.

1. *Anata wa mainiti nani wo simasu ka.* 2. *Watakusi wa mainiti shomotu yomimasu* (read). 3. *Anata no tomodati wa mainiti nani wo simasu ka.* 4. *Watakusi no tomodati wa mainiti ye wo kakimasu* (paints). 5. *Anata no kiodai wa konniti koko ye kimasu ka.* 6. *Watakusi no kiodai wa konniti koko ye kimasu.* 7. *Anata wa kono saiku wo mimasita ka.* 8. *Watakusi wa mada* (yet) *kono saiku wo mimasenanda.* 9. *Anata wa kore wo dō omoimasu* (think of) *ka.* 10. *Watakusi wa sore ni kanzimasu.* 11. *Zinmin wo kioiku suru gu yō gozarimasu.* 12. *Anata wa kono saiku ni kanzimasu ka.* 13. *Watakusi wa sono saiku ni kanzimasu.* 14. *Anata wa konniti watakusi no iye ye kimasu ka.* 15. *Watakusi wa konniti anata no iye ye ikimasen.*

LXXXIV.

1. Who comes here? 2. Your brother comes here. 3. Do you not know my name? 4. I do not know your name. 5. Do you admire this workmanship? 6. I admire this workmanship. 7. What do you do to-day? 8. I read my books to-day. 9. Where do you go? 10. I go to Asakusa. 11. Do you like pictures? 12. I like pictures.

LXXXV.

Indicative Mood. Past.

Kimasita, came, or has or have come.
Simasita, did, or has or have done.
Kioiku simasita, educated, or has or have educated.
Kimasenanda, has or have not come.
Simasenanda, has or have not done.

Sibai or *Sibaya,* theatre. | *Sitateya,* tailor.
Tera, church. | *Kutuya,* shoemaker.

1. *Anata wa koko ye itu kimasita ka.* 2. *Watakusi wa koko ye sakuzitu kimasita.* 3. *Sakuzitu anata wa nani wo simasita ka.* 4. *Sakuzitu watakusi wa shomotu wa yomimasita.* 5. *Anata wa konniti sibai ye ikimasu ka.* 6. *Watakusi wa konniti tera ye ikimasu.* 7. *Dare ga kimamasita ka.* 8. *Sitateya ga kimasita.* 9. *Anata wa kimono wo kosirayemasu* (make) *ka.* 10. *Watakusi wa haori wo kosirayemasu.* 11. *Anata wa konchō nani wo simasita ka.* 12. *Watakusi wa konchō sinbunsi* (newspaper) *mo yomimasita.* 13. *Anata wa kono saiku ni kanzimasita ka.* 14. *Watakusi wa kono saiku ni kanzimasita.*

LXXXVI.

1. Where did you go yesterday? 2. I went to Asakusa. 3. Did you read the newspaper yesterday? 4. I read the newspaper yesterday. 5. Did you come to my

house last night (*saku ya*)? 6. I came to your house last night, but you were not at home. 7. Did you go to church this morning? 8. Who came here yesterday? 9. A shoemaker came here yesterday. 10. Yesterday a tailor came here. 11. Do you make a coat? 12. I make a cloak (tonbi). 13. Do you come here every morning? 14. I come here every morning.

LXXXVII.

Indicative Mood. Future.

Kimasho, shall or will come.
Simasho, shall or will do or make.
Kanzimasho, will or shall admire.
Kimasumai, will or shall not come.
Simasumai, will or shall not do or make.

1. *Itu anata no tomodati wa koko ye kimasho ka.* 2. *Watakusi no tomodati wa koko ye kimasumai.* 3. *Dokoye anata wa ikimasu ka.* 4. *Watakusi wa konniti Yokohama ya ikimasu.* 5. *Nani wo watakusi wa miyo niti simasho ka.* 6. *Anata wa miyo niti tera ye ikimasho.* 7. *Konniti anata no kiodai wa watakusi no iye ye kimasumai ka.* 8. *Watakusi no kiodai wa konniti anata no iye ye kimasumai.* 9. *Anata wa mainiti nani wo simasu ka.* 10. *Watakusi wa mainiti shomotu wo yomimasu.* 11. *Anata no tomodati wa mainiti gakkō* (school) *ye ikimasu ka.* 12. *Watakusi no tomodati wa*

Japanese and English Exercises.

mainiti gakkō ye ikimasen. 13. *Sono okata wa kono saiku ni kanzimasho ka.* 14. *Kono okata wa sono saiku ni kanzimasho.* 15. *Anata wa watakusi no tomodati wo itu mimasita ka.* 16. *Watakusi wa anata no tomodati wo sakusitu mimasita.* 17. *Tenki ga yō gozarimasu.*

LXXXVIII.

1. What did you do yesterday? 2. I went to Yokohama. 3. What does your brother do every day? 4. My brother goes to school every day. 5. Where are you going? 6. I am going to Asakusa. 7. When will your friend come to my house? 8. My friend will come to your house to-morrow evening. 9. Do you go to church often (*tabitabi*)? 10. I go to church sometimes (*toki-doki*). 11. Will your brother admire this workmanship if (he) sees (it)*? 12. My brother will admire this workmanship. 13. Shall we go to Yokohama to-night. 14. My brother will go to Yokohama to-morrow evening. 15. Do you like tea? 16. I like tea. 17. Do you drink saké? 18. I drink saké.

LXXXIX.

Mattu, to wait.
Utaū, to sing.
Konomu, to like.
Hanasu, speak.

Usinau, to lose.
Kaku, to write, or to paint.
Uru, to sell.

* Here nominative and objective are understood in the Japanese sentence.

In conversation,* relative pronouns are always understood; thus, *Sore wa watakusi ga mimasita hito de gozarimasu,* He is the man whom I have seen; *Sore wa watakusi no iye ni kimasita hito de gozarimasu,* He is the man who came to my house.

Nasi, pear.
Kudamono, fruit.
Mikan, orange.
Uta, song.
Tegami, letter.

Igilisu kotoba, English language.
Furansu kotoba, French language.

1. *Anata wa tegami wo kakimasita ka.* 2. *Watakusi wa tegami wo kakimasita.* 3. *Kore wa anata ga mimasita shomotu de gozarimasu ka.* 4. *Kore wa watakusi ga mimasita shomotu de gozarimasu.* 5. *Anata wa dokoye ikimasu ka.* 6. *Watakusi wa anata ga sakuzitu ikimasita tokoro* (the place) *ye ikimasu.* 7. *Anata wa uta wo utaimasu ka.* 8. *Watakusi wa uta wo utaimasen ga* (but) *watakusi no musume ga utaimasu.* 9. *Anata no tomodati wa nashi wo konomimasu ka.* 10. *Watakusi no tomodati wa mikan wo konomimasu.* 11. *Sono okata wa Igilisu kotoba wo hanasimasu ka.* 12. *Kono okata wa Furansu kotoba wo hanasimasu.* 13. *Anata wa kokode dare wo mattimasu ka.* 14. *Watakusi wa kokode watakusi no tomodati wo mattimasu.* 15. *Anata wa kudamono wo konomimasu ka.* 16. *Watakusi wa kudamono wo konomimasen ga watakusi no musume ga konomimasu.* 17. *Dare*

* See Rule XII.

ga kono shomotu wo urimasu ka. 18. *Shomotuya* (bookseller) *ga kono shomotu wo urimasu.*

XC.

1. Does your brother speak the French language? 2. My brother speaks the English language. 3. Did you write your letters' last night? 4. I did not write my letters last night, but my brother wrote (them). 5. Is that the man whom you saw yesterday? 6. That is the man whom I saw yesterday. 7. Does your friend like oranges? 8. My friend likes oranges. 9. Is this the man who sells cloth? 10. This is the man who sells cloth. 11. Do you wait here for your brother? 12. I wait here for my daughter. 13. How much does this book cost (*simasu*)? 14. This book costs three shillings (*san bu*). 15. Does your friend sing a song? 16. My friend does not sing a song.

XCI.

To .... to, and.
Keredomo, but.
Watakusi no, mine.
Atai, price.

Iro, colour.
Kireina, kireini, beautiful
Hanahada, very.
Mairimasu, go, or goes.

1. *Watakusi to watakusi no kiodai to ga konniti Asakusa ye mairimasu* (go). 2. *Watakusi wa Igilisu kotoba wo hanasimasen keredomo watakusi no kiodai ga*

hanasimasu. 3. *Anata wa ima doko ni orimasu ka.* 4. *Watakusi wa ima Yokohama ni orimasu.* 5. *Kono shomotu wa anata no de gozarimasu ka.* 6. *Kono shomotu wa watakusi no kiodai no de gozarimasu.* 7. *Kono shomotu wa watakusi no de gozarimasen.* 8. *Kono tanmono no atai wa ikura de gozarimasu ka.* 9. *Kono tanmono no atai wa go riyo de gozarimasu.* 10. *Anata no kimono no iro wa kireini gozarimasu.* 11. *Anata no niwa ni arimasu hana wa hanahada kireini gozarimasu.* 12. *Anata no tomodati wa watakusi no niwa wo mimasita ka.* 13. *Watakusi no tomodati wa mada* (yet) *anata no niwa wo mimasenanda.* 14. *Sakuzitu anata wa nani wo simasita ka.* 15. *Sakuzitu watakusi wa tomodati no iye ye ikimasita.* 16. *Anata no tomodati wa dokoni orimasu ka.* 17. *Watakusi no tomodati wa Yedo ni orimasu.* 18. *Anata wa konniti tegami wo anata no tomodati ye okurimasu* (send) *ka.* 19. *Watakusi wa konniti tegami wo watakusi no haha ni okurimasu.* 20. *Konchō anata wa sinbunsi* (newspaper) *wo mimasita ka.* 21. *Watakusi wa konchō mada sinbunsi wo mimasenanda.*

XCII.

1. The flowers (which) are in your garden are very beautiful. 2. Do you like flowers? 3. I like flowers. 4. Where do you go to? 5. I go to my friend's house. 6. What do you do every day? 7. I read books every day. 8. Did you receive my letter yesterday? 9. I

received your letter this morning. 10. I do not like those pictures, but my friends like (them). 11. This is the workmanship (which) I saw three years ago. 12. Who came here to day ? 13. The tailor and draper (*tanmonoya*) came here to-day. 14. How much does this cloth cost ? 15. That cloth costs three riyo. 16. Will your friends come to your house this evening ? 17. My friends will come to my house this evening.

XCIII.

Mosi....nara, if.	*Tatoye....nisiro* or *sitemo,* although.

Mosi watakusi ga sono okata wo mimasita nara kono tegami wo watasimasho. If I see him, (I) shall deliver letter (to him).

Tatoye konniti wa yoi tenki de gozarimasu nisiro, miyoniti wa uten de gozarimasho. Although it may be fine to-day, yet to-morrow it will rain.

Onasi or *Onazi, koto* or *mono,* the same thing.	*Konniti wa,** good day.
Kinu, silk.	*Sayo* or *hei,* yes.
Sazi, spoon.	*Iye* or *Iya,* no.
Sayōnara, good-bye.	*Wasuremasita,* has or have forgotten or forgot.

* *Konniti wa yoi tenki de gozarimasu,* "This day is a fine day," is contracted into *Konniti wa.*

1. Mosi watakusi ga konniti anata no tomodati wo mimasita nara, kono kinu wo watasimasho. 2. Anata no shomotu to watakusi no wa onazi koto de gozarimasu ka. 3. Iye watakusi no shomotu to anata no wa onasi koto de gozarimasen. 4. Anata wa konniti gakkō ye ikimasenanda ka. 5. Hei watakusi wa konniti gakko ye ikimasenanda.* 6. Naze (why) anata no tomodati wa konniti watakusi no iye ye kimasen ka. 7. Watakusi no tomodati wa konnchō Yedo ye ikimasita kara anata no tokoro ye kimasen. 8. Anata wa kono kinu wo ikura ni kaimesita ka. 9. Watakusi wa sono kinu wo itt shaku (one foot) ni riyo ni kaimasita. 10. Anata wa London ni orimasita ka. 11. Hei watakusi wa London ni san nen orimasita. 12. Anata wa Igilisu no kikō (English climate) wo konomimasen ka. 13. Hei watakusi wa Igilisu no kiko wo konomimasen. 14. Itu mata (again) anata wa Yedo ye ikimasu ka. 15. Miyoniti watakusi wa Yedo ye ikimasu. 16. Watakusi wa konniti tegami wo watakusi no haha kara uketorimasita. 17. Mai tuki (every month) anata wa tegami wo anata no tomodati ni okurimasu ka. 18. Hei watakusi wa mai tuki tegami wo watakusi no tomodati ni okurimasu.

XCIV.

1. Although it is fine now, it will rain presently (*imani*). 2. Have you forgotten me? 3. No, I have

* Here is the difference between yes and *hei*.

not forgotten you. 4. Where are you living now? 5. I am living in Yedo. 6. When are you coming to my house? 7. I am going to your house to-day. 8. Have you bought this silk? 9. Yes, I bought that silk. 10. How much did that cost? 11. This cost three riyo a foot (*itt shaku*). 12. If I see your friend to-day, what shall I say (to him)? 13. If you see my friend to-day, deliver (*watasite kudasare*) this letter (to him). 14. Did you live in England a long time (*nagaku*)? 15. I lived in England three years. 16. I have lost my book.

XCV.

Yakusoku suru, To promise, to make an agreement.

The word *to* (with) must be put after the names of persons to whom we make a promise.

Watakusi wa kono okata to miyo niti Yedo ye iku yakusoku simasita. I promised you to go to Yedo to-morrow.

Watasu, to deliver. | *Shabon,* soap.
Tou, to ask. | *Tenugui,* towel.

1. *Anata wa konchō anata no tomodati ni tegami wo okurimasita ka.* 2. *Watakusi wa tegami wo sakuzitu okurimasita.* 3. *Anata wa kono kane wo dare ni watasimasu ka.* 4. *Watakusi wa kono kane wo watakusi no tomodati ni okurimasu.* 5. *Itu anata wa sono kane wo kono okata ni watasimasita ka.* 6. *Sakuzitu watakusi wa*

sono kane wo kono okata ni watasimasita. 7. *Anata wa sono koto wo anata no tomodati ni toimasita ka.* 8. *Iye watakusi wa sono koto wo mada toimasenanda.* 9. *Anata wa watakusi no segare to miyo niti Yedo ye iku yakusoku simasita ka.* 10. *Iye watakusi wa anata no tomodati to Yokohama ye iku yakusoku simasita.* 11. *Sakuya anatagata wa sibai ye ikimasita ka.* 12. *Iye watakusi domo wa sakuzitu Asakusa ye ikimasita.* 13. *Annta wa konniti tegami wo anata no kuni* (country) *kara uketorimasita ka.* 14. *Sayo, watakusi wa tegami wo watakusi no haha kara uketorimasita.*

XCVI.

1. From whom did you receive this letter? 2. I received that letter from my father. 3. How much did your horse cost? 4. My horse cost 100 riyo. 5. Where are you going to-day? 6. We are going to Yokohama. 7. What do you do every day? 8. I read books every day? 9. Where do you live now? 10. I live in Yedo. 11. To whom do you send that letter? 12. I send that letter to my father. 13. Did you promise that person to go to Yedo to-day? 14. No, I did not promise that person to go to Yedo to-day. 15. Did you ask your brother (about) this matter? 16. No, I have not asked my brother (about) this matter yet (*mada*).

Japanese and English Exercises.

XCVII.

In the Japanese, when we apply *ko* (son), *kanai* (wife), and *kiodai* (brother) to those of others, we prefix *o* or *go* before these words merely to express our respect to others.

Watakusi no ko, my son.
Anata no o ko [special courtesy], your son.
Watakusi no kinai, my wife.
Anata no go kanai [special courtesy], your wife.

Noru, to ride.	*Jōkisen*, steamer.
Kayeru, to return.	*Jōkisha*, railway train.

1. *Watakusi wa konniti anata no go kanai wo mimasita.* 2. *Anata wa doko de watakusi no kanai wo mimasita ka.* 3. *Watakusi wa anata no go kanai wo jōkisha de mimasita.* 4. *Anata wa konniti Yokohama kara jokisha de kimasita ka mata* (or) *jōkisen de kimasita ka.* 5. *Watakusi wa jōkisha de kimasita.* 6. *Anata no o ko wa ikutu de gozarimasu ka.* 7. *Watakusi no ko wa zu ni de gozarimasu.* 8. *Anata wa jōkisha ni noru koto wo konomimasu ka.* 9. *Iye, watakusi wa jōkisha ni noru koto wo konomimasen.* 10. *Anata no go kiodai wa konniti doko ye ikimasita ka.* 11. *Watakusi no kiodai wa konniti Yedo ye ikimasita.* 12. *Kono okata wa anata no otomodati de gozarimasu ka.* 13. *Sayo, kono okata wa watakusi no tomodati de gozarimasu.* 14. *Anata no kuni ni jōkisha ga gozarimasu ka.* 15. *Hei, watakusi no kuni ni jōkisha ga gozarimasu.*

XCVIII.

1. Did you come here by a train or steamer? 2. I came by a steamer. 3. Are there railways in your country? 4. There is a railway in my country. 5. Is your wife in your house? 6. No, my wife went to Yokohama. 7. Is that your brother? 8. No, that is my friend. 9. I have seen your daughter in Asakusa. 10. When did you see my daughter in Asakusa? 11. I saw your daughter three days ago. 12. When will your brother return from Kanagawa? 13. My brother will return to-day. 14. Did you ride in the train often (*tabitabi*). 15. No, I rode in the train three times (*san do*).

XCIX.

When we apply *haha* (mother) and *titi* (father) to those of others, we add the word *sama*, or sometimes we use altogether different words: — *Okkasan* for mother, and *ottossan* for father.

Anata no titisama or *ottossan*, your father.
Watakusi no haha or *titi*, my mother, or father.

Oji, uncle.
Asa-mesi, breakfast.
Hiru-mesi, dinner.
Ban-mesi, supper.

Oba, aunt.
Taberu, to eat.
Nomu, to drink.
Sakana, fish.

Japanese and English Exercises. 91

1. Watakusi wa sakuzitu anata no hahasama wo mimasita. 2. Anata wa doko de watakusi no haha wo mimasita ka. 3. Watakusi wa anata no okkasan wo Asakusa de mimasita. 4. Anata wa konchō asa-meshi wo tabemasita ka. 5. Hei watakusi wa konchō asa-meshi wo tabemasita. 6. Anata wa ban-meshi ni itudemo (always) saké wo nomimasu ka. 7. Īye, watakusi wa ban-meshi ni cha wo nomimasu. 8. Anata wa hiru-meshi ni nani wo tabemasu ka. 9. Watakusi wa hiru-meshi ni sakana to niku wo tabemasu. 10. Konniti anata no titisama or ottossan wa doko ye ikimasita ka. 11. Watakusi no titi wa Yedo ye ikimasita. 12. Anata no hahasama wa itu Yedo kara kayerimasu ka. 13. Miyo niti watakusi no haha wa kayerimasu. 14. Kore wa anata no ojisama de gozarimasu ka. 15. Hei kore wa watakusi no oji de gozarimasu. 16. Sono okata wa anata no obasama de gozarimasu ka. 17. Hei kono okata wa watakusi no oba de gozarimasu. 18. Anata wa konniti Yedo ye ikimasen ka. 19. Hei watakusi wa ikmasen.*

C.

1. Where is your brother? 2. My brother is in the house. 3. I have seen your mother in the garden. 4. Did you finish (*sumimasita*) your breakfast? 5. Yes, I finished my breakfast. 6. At what time does your

* In some cases *Hei* and *Īye* do not correspond to the English 'yes' and 'no'; or, as the examples above show, there is a difference in the idiomatic use of these words in the two languages.

father get up? 7. My father gets up at seven o'clock. 8. What do you eat at dinner? 9. I eat meat and fish. 10. Does your mother like meat? 11. My mother likes meat. 12. At what time do you eat supper? .13. I eat supper at six o'clock. 14. Do you write a letter to your father every day? 15. Yes, I write a letter to my father every day. 16. Will your brother return here to-day? 17. I do not know (*zouzimasen*). 18. Have you seen the railway trains? 19. Yes, I rode in the train often (*tabitabi*).

CI.

Sosiraremasu, is, or are sneered at.
Sosiraremasita, was, or were sneered at.
Wutaremasu, is, or are beaten.
Wutaremasita, was, or were beaten.
Miraremasu, is, or are seen or looked at.
Miraremasita, was, or were seen or looked at.

Hana mi ni, to see the flower.
Fune, ship, or boat.
Inu, dog.
Sono hito, that person.
Kawa, river.

Sakura, cherry-tree, or flower.
Sakuzitu, yesterday.
Mati, street.
Kisi, bank.
Fuzin, lady.

1. *Kono inu wa hito ni wutaremasu ka.* 2. *Iye, kno inu wa hito ni wutaremasen.* 3. *Sono inu wa sakuzitu hito ni wutaremasita.* 4. *Sono fuzin wa hito ni mi-*

Japanese and English Exercises. 93

raremasu ka. 5. *Kono fuzin wa sakuzitu hito ni miraremasita.* 6. *Dokode sono fuzin wa hito ni miraremasita ka.* 7. *Mati de miraremasita.* 8. *Itudemo kireina fuzin wa hito ni miraremasu.* 9. *Anata wa hana mini ikimasita ka.* 10. *Watakusi wa fune de hana mini ikimasita.* 11. *Sakura wa doko ni gozarimasu ka.* 12. *Sakura wa kawa no kisi ni gozarimasu.* 13. *Sakura wa fune kara miraremasu ka.* 14. *Hei fune kara miraremasu.* 15. *Sakura wa kireina hana de gozarimasu ka.* 16. *Sakura wa hanada kireini gozarimasu.* 17. *Sono fuzin wa hito ni sosiraremasu ka.* 18. *Iye, kono fuzin wa hito ni homeraremasu* (is praised). 19. *Sono hito wa hito ni homeraremasu ka matawa sosiraremasu ka.* 20. *Kono hito wa hito ni homeraremasu.* 21. *Mainiti tenki ga yō gozarimasu kara, sakura no hana ga kireini gozarimasho.* 22. *Dare ga hana mini ikimasu ka.* 23. *Watakusi no tomodati to watakusi ga hana mini ikimasu.* 24. *Hana wa doko ni takusan arimasu ka.* 25. *Muko zima ni arimasu.*

CII.

1. Was this lady seen by the people yesterday? 2. Yes, this lady was seen by the people. 3. Where was that lady seen by the people? 3. This beautiful lady was seen by the people everywhere (*dokodemo*). 5. Where did you go yesterday? 6. I went to see the flower. 7. Where is the flower? 8. (It) is on the bank of a river. 9. When did you go to the theatre?

10. I went to the theatre yesterday. 11. Was that person sneered at by the people? 12. No, that person was not sneered at by the people. 13. How did you go to see the flower? 14. I went in a boat. 15. Who was beaten yesterday? 16. This dog was beaten yesterday. 17. Do you write a letter to-morrow? 18. I write a letter to-morrow. 19. Are (there) cherry-trees in the street? 20. Yes, there are cherry-trees in the street. 21. The flower of a cherry-tree is beautiful. 22. I do not go to see the flower, but my friend goes.

CIII.

Miyemasu,
Miru koto ga dekimasu, } can see.

Ikemasu,
Iku koto ga dekimasu, } can go.

Yomemasu,
Yomu koto ga dekimasu, } can read.

Kakemasu,
Kaku koto ga dekimasu, } can paint, or write.

Mono, thing.
Tōku, } distance.
Yenpo, }
Musi, insect.

Tada ima, just now.
Yozi, business.
Megane, spectacle.
Saka duki, saké cup.

1. *Konniti sibai ye anata wa ikemasu ka.* 2. *Hei, watakusi wa konniti sibai ye iku koto ga dekimasu.* 3. *Anata wa kono tisana musi wo miru koto ga deki-*

masu ka. 4. *Īye, sono musi wa miyemasen.* 5. *Anata wa yenpo ga miyemasu ka.* 6. *Watakusi wa megane nasini yenpo ga miyemasen.* 7. *Anata wa tada ima Yokohama ye iku koto ga dekimasu ka.* 8. *Watakusi wa itudemo ikemasu.* 9. *Konniti anata wa hana mini iku koto ga dekimasu ka.* 10. *Watakusi wa konniti hana mini iku koto ga dekimasu.* 11. *Anata wa kono tisai mono wo megane nasini miru koto ga dekimasu ka.* 12. *Īye, watakusi wa megane nasini sore wo miru koto ga dekimasen.* 13. *Izen anata wa dokoni orimasita. ka.* 14. *Watakusi wa izen Nagasaki ni orimasita.* 15. *Mata anata wa Nagasaki ye ikimasu ka.* 16. *Hei, watakusi wa, yozi ga arimasu kara, Nagasaki ye ikimasu.* 17. *Anata wa Nagasaki kara hayaku kayeru koto ga dekimasu.* 18. *Īye, watakusi wa hayaku kayeru koto ga dekimasen.* 19. *Sokoni sakaduki ga arimasu ka.* 20. *Īye, kokoni sakaduki wa arimasen.* 21. *Anata wa kono shomotu wo yomu koto ga dekimasu ka.* 22. *Īye, watakusi wa sono shomotu wo yomu koto ga dekimasen.* 23. *Anata wa ye ga kakemasu ka.* 24. *Watakusi wa ye ga kakemasu.*

CIV.

1. Have you any buisness to-day? 2. No, I have not any business. 3. Can you go to Asakusa this morning? 4. I can go (there) just now. 5. Can you read this book? I can read that book. 7. Can you write

a letter to-day? 8. Yes, I can write a letter to-day. 9. Can you see this small insect without spectacles? 10. Yes, I can see (it). 11. Where do you go every day? 12. I go to see the flower every day. 13. Can you go to see the flower every morning? 14. I can go to see the flower every morning. 15. Was this dog beaten by the people last night? 16. Yes, this dog was beaten last night. 17. Can you paint a picture? 18. Yes, I can paint a picture. 19. Can you go to Nagasaki in a ship? 20. Yes, I can go to Nagasaki in a ship. 21. Can you see that? 22. I can see that. 23. Can you read this English word?- 24. Yes, I can read (it).

CV.

Ikemasita, *Iku koto ga dekimasita,*	could go.
Ikemasen, *Iku koto ga dekimasen,*	cannot go.
Miyemasen, *Miru koto ga dekimasen,*	cannot see.

Kumo, spider.	*Tōmegane,* telescope.
Inaka, country.	*Hai,* fly.
Turi, fishing.	*Hane,* wing.
Kenbikiyo, microscope.	*Asi,* foot, or feet.

1. *Anata wa konniti sibai ye ikemasu ka.* 2. *Iye, watakusi wa konniti ikemasen.* 3. *Anata wa sakuzitu*

Asakusa ye iku koto ga dekimasita ka. 4. *Hei, dekimasita.* / 5. *Anata wa kono hai wo kenbi kiyo de mimasita ka.* 6. *Watakusi wa sono hai no hane wo kenbikiyo de mimasita.* 7. *Anata wa sono hane wo yoku miru koto ga dekimasita ka.* 8. *Hei, watakusi wa sore wo yoku miru koto ga dekimasita.* 9. *Watakusi wa kumo no asi wo kenbikiyo nasini yoku miru koto ga dekimasen.* 10. *Anata wo koncho inaka ye iku koto ga dekimasu ka.* 11. *Iye, koncho watakusi wa iku koto ga dekimasen.* 12. *Anata wa mainiti turi ni iku koto ga dekimasu ka.* 13. *Iye, watakusi wa mainiti turini iku koto wa dekimasen.* 14. *Itu anata wa inaka ye iku koto ga dekimasu ka.* 15. *Koncho watakusi wa ikimasu.* 16. *Anata wa nani wo tōmegane de mimasu ka.* 17. *Watakusi wa tōmegane de hosi wo mimasu.* 18. *Anata wa sore wo tōmegane nasi ni miru koto ga dekimasu ka.* 19. *Watakusi wa tomegane nasi ni miru koto ga dekimasu.* 20. *Anata wa sakuzitu hana mini iku koto ga dekimasita.* 21. *Sakuzitu hana mini iku koto ga dekimasita.* 22. *Anata wa kono musi no asi wo kenbikiyo de miru koto ga dekimasita ka.* 23. *Hei, miru koto ga dekimasita.* 24. *Anata wa kono shomotu wo yomu koto ga dekimasita ka.* 25. *Hei, sono shomotu wo yomu koto ga dekimasita.*

CVI.

1. Could you go to a tailor yesterday? 2. Yes, I could go to a tailor yesterday. 3. When did you go

H

to a shoemaker? 4. I went to a shoemaker yesterday. 5. Could you see this small wing with a microscope? 6. Yes, I saw it with a microscope. 7. Why could you not go to see the flower yesterday? 8. I could not go to see the flower yesterday, because I had business (or there was business). 9. How did you go to Nagasaki? 10. I went in a ship. 11. At what time can you go to Yokohama to-day? 12. I can go to Yokohama directly. 13. Can you see this small work without a microscope? 14. No, I cannot see this small work without a microscope. 15. Have you seen the wing of a fly with a microscope? 16. Yes, I have seen (it). 17. Can you see the foot of a spider well without a microscope? 18. No, I cannot see (it) well. 19. When you were in Japan, did you go to Asakusa? 20. Yes, when I was in Japan, I went to Asakusa. 21. When you were in Japan, were you able to go to see the flower? 22. When I was in Tokio, I went in a boat to see the flower. 23. Was this small dog beaten by the people yesterday? 24. No, this small dog was not beaten.

CVIII.

Miyemasho, *Miru koto ga dekimasho,*	Will, or shall be able to see.
Miyemasumai, *Miru koto ga dekimasumai,*	Will, or shall not be able to see.

Japanese and English Exercises.

Ikemasho, } Will, or shall be able
Iku koto ga dekimasho, } to go.
Ikemasumai, } Will, or shall not be
Iku koto ga dekimasumai, } able to go.

Kaze, wind.	*Koye,* sound, or voice.
Kiku, chrysanthemum.	*Tori,* bird.
Yuri, lily.	*Wuguisu,* nightingale.
Ayame, sweet flag.	*Wataru,* to cross.
Kakitubata, iris.	*Sewashū,* busy.

1. *Miyoniti watakusi wa yuri no hana wo miru koto ga dekimasho ka.* 2. *Hei, Anata wa miyoniti yuri no hana wo miru koto ga dekimasho.* 3. *Nitiyoniti ni watakusi wa sono ye wo miru koto ga dekimasho ka.* 4. *Iye, nitiyoniti ni wa miru koto ga dekimasen ga getuyoniti ni dekimasho.* 5. *Asakusa ye watakusi wa miyoniti fune de iku koto ga dekimasho ka.* 6. *Hei, dekimasho.* 7. *Wumi wo fune de wataru koto ga dekimasu ka.* 8. *Konniti anata wa fune de wataru koto ga dekimasen.* 9. *Miyoniti fune de wumi wo wataru koto ga dekimasho ka.* 10. *Hei, Miyoniti anata wa fune de wataru koto ga dekimasho.* 11. *Naze konniti wataru koto ga dekimasen.* 12. *Konniti wa kaze ga tuyō gozarimasu kara, dekimasen.* 13. *Anata wa tokei wo kosirayeru koto ga dekimasu ka.* 14. *Hei, watakusi wa tokei wo kosirayeru koto ga dekimasu.* 15. *Anata wa Nipon no kotoba wo hanasu koto ga dekimasu ka.* 16. *Watakusi wa Nipon no kotoba wo sukosi hanasu koto ga*

dekimasu. 17. *Miyoniti watakusi domo wa kiku no hana wo miru koto ga dekimasho ka.* 18. *Anata gata wa miyoniti kiku no hana wo miru koto ga dekimasumai.* 19. *Anata wa konnen* (this year) *wuguisu no koye wo kikimasita ka.* 20. *Haru* (Spring) *ga kimasen kara, mada watakusi wa wuguisu no koye wo kikimasen.* 21. *Anata wa ayame no hana wo mimasita ka.* 22. *Iye, mada watakusi wa ayame wo mimasen ga kakitubata wo mimasita.*

CVIII.

1. Will you be able to go to the theatre to-morrow?
2. Yes, I shall be able to go to the theatre to-morrow.
3. Will your friend be able to go to Sinagawa to-morrow morning (*miyocho*)?
4. Yes, my friend will be able to go to Sinagawa to-morrow morning.
5. Will you be able to see that bird to-morrow?
6. Yes, I shall be able to see that bird to-morrow.
7. Will you be able to see that lily to-morrow evening?
8. Yes, I shall be able to see that lily.
9. Shall we be able to hear the voice of a nightingale in this place (*koko de*)?
10. You will not be able to hear the voice of a nightingale here.
11. Shall we be able to cross the sea to-day?
12. You will be able to cross the sea if there is no wind.
13. Will you be able to read this book to-morrow?
14. No, I shall not be able to read that book, because I am busy.
15. Will you be able

Japanese and English Exercises. 101

to see this wing of a fly with a microscope to-morrow?
16. I shall be able to do so (*Dekimasho*). 17. Shall we be able to go to Mukozima in a boat to-morrow? 18. We shall be able to go to Mukozima in a boat to-morrow. 19. Have you seen that beautiful bird? 20. I have seen that beautiful bird. 21. Will you be able to go to Sikoku next year? 22. We shall not be able to go to Sikoku next year.

CIX.

Mosi . . . nara, if.
Miyo, see (command).
Mite kudasare, pray see (entreaty).
Ike, go (command).
Ite kudasare, pray go (entreaty).

Iku koto, to go.
Miru koto, } to see.
Mini,* }
Yomu koto, } to read.
Yomini.* }
Kiku koto, } to hear.
Kikini,* }

1. *Sore wo miyo.* 2. *Sore wo mite kudasare.* 3. *Soko ye ike.* 4. *Soko ye ite kudasare.* 5. *Anata wa Yokohama ye ikimasu nara, watakusi no tomodati no iye ye ite kudasare.* 6. *Anata wa konniti yōzi ga gozarimasen nara, watakusi no shomotu wo mite kudasare.* 7. *Anata wa hanasi wo kiku koto wo sukimasu ka.* 8. *Hei, watakusi wa hanasi wo kiku koto wo sukimasu.* 9. *Anata wa itu hanasi wo kikini ikimasu*

* This form of the infinitive mood is used when it is governed by an intransitive verb.

ka. 10. Watakusi wa hanasi wo maiban kikini ikimasu.
11. Anata wa sibai ye iku koto wo sukimasu ka.
12. Hei, watakusi wa sibai ye iku koto wo sukimasu.
13. Nipon no fuzin wa sibai ye iku koto wo sukimasu ka. 14. Hei, Nipon no fuzin wa sibai ye iku koto wo suki masu. 15. Hanasi wo kiku koto wa hanahada yō gozarimasu. 16. Sibai wo miru koto wa hanahada omosirō gazarimasu. 17. Shomotu wo yomu koto wa hanahada taisetu de gozarimasu (important). 18. Anata wa doko ye shomotu wo yomini ikimasu ka.
19. Watakusi wa shomotu wo yomini gakko ye ikimasu.
20. Anata wa gakko ye iku koto wo sukimasu ka.
21. Hei, watakusi wa gakko ye iku koto wo sukimasu.
22. Anata wa wuguisu no koye wo kiku koto sukimasu ka. 23. Watakusi wa wuguisu no koye wo kiku koto wo sukimasu. 24. Anata wa kenbikiyo de tisai mono wo miru koto wo sukimasu ka. 25. Kenbikiyo de tisai musi wo miru koto wa omosiro gozarimasu.

CX.

1. Do you like to read books? 2. Yes, I like to read books. 3. What book do you like to read? 4. I like to read a novel (*kusazosi*). 5. To read a novel is amusing, but to read a history (*rekisi*) is important. 6. Go to the left. 7. See that man. 8. Do you often go to (see) a theatre? 9. I do not go to (see) the theatre often. But I like to go to the

Japanese and English Exercises. 103

theatre. 10. Does your friend like to hear an amusing story? 11. Yes, my friend likes to hear an amusing story. 12. Will you be able to go to hear a story to-day? 13. No, I shall not be able to do so. 14. Will you be able to go to see the flower to-morrow morning? 15. I shall not be able to do so. 16. Why can you not go to the theatre this evening? 17 I cannot go to the theatre to-day, because I have business (there is business). 18. If you go to Asakusa, pray go to the house of my brother. 19. If you come to my house, pray see my picture. 20. Pray see that book. 21. Where do you go to read books? 22. I go to read books in the school. 23. Do you like to go to the school every day. 24. Yes, I like to do so.

CXI.

Oide nasare,	go.
Oide nasareta,	went.
Oide nasaren,	does, or do not go.
Oide nasarenanda,	did not go.

These forms of the verb are employed to address the second person when respect is expressed. For instance, *Dokoye anata wa oide nasaru ka* instead of *Doko ye anata wa ikimasu ka*. Where do you go? The latter way of expression is quite intelligible, but the former is preferable as a mere polite expression.

104   Japanese and English Exercises.

Goran nasaru,	see.
Goran nasaren,	does, or do not see.
Okiki nasaru,	hear.
Okiki nasaren,	does, or do not hear.
Oyomi nasaru,	read.
Oyomi nasaren,	does, or do not read.
Owuketori nasaru,	receive.
Owuketori nasaren,	does, or do not receive.
Okomomi nasaru,	like.
Okonomi nasaren,	does, or do not like.
Okosiraye nasaru,	make.
Okosiraye nasaren,	does, or do not make.
Onomi nasaru,	drink.
Onomi nasaren,	does, or do not drink.
Okirai nasaru,	dislike.
Okirai nasaren,	does, or do not like.
Otadune nasaru,	seek, or look for.
Otadune nasaren,	does, or do not seek.
Okangaye nasaru,	think.
Okangaye nasaren,	does, or do not think.

1. Anata wa koncho doko ye oide nasaru ka. 2. Watakusi wa Yokohama ye ikimasu. 3. Anata wa konniti Asakusa ye oide nasaru ka. 4. Iye, konniti watakusi wa ikimasen. 5. Anata wa sakuzitu Sinagawa ye oide nasareta ka. 6. Iye, watakusi wa sakutzitu Sinagawa ye ikimasenanda. 7. Anata wa konban Kanagawa ye oide nasaru ka. 8. Iye, watakusi wa konban Kanagawa

Japanese and English Exercises. 105

ye ikimasen. 9. *Anata wa nani wo sakuzitu goran nasareta ka.* 10. *Watakusi wa sakuzitu hana wo mimasita.* 11. *Anata wa sakuzitu omosiroi hanasi wo okiki nasareta ka.* 12. *Hei, sakuzitu watakusi wa omosiroi hanasi wo kikimasita.* 13. *Konniti anata wa shomotu wo oyomi nasaru ka.* 14. *Hei, watakusi wa shomotu wo yomimasu.* 15. *Konncho anata wa watakusi no tegami wo owuketori nasareta ka.* 16. *Hei, watakusi wa anata no otegami wo koncho wuketorimasita.* 17. *Anata wa sibai ye iku koto wo okonomina saru ka.* 18. *Watakusi wa sibai ye iku koto wo konomimasu.* 19. *Anata ga kono kireina hako wo okosiraye nasareta ka.* 20. *Hei, watakusi ga kosirayemasita.* 21. *Anata wa sake wo onominasaru ka.* 22. *Iye, watakusi wa sake wo nomimasen.* 23. *Anata wa kono tisai inu wo okirai nasaru ka.* 24. *Iye, watakusi wa sono inu wo sukimasu.* 25. *Soko de anata wa nani wo otadune nasaru ka.* 26. *Watakusi wa watakusi no tomodati no shomotu wo tadune masu.*

CXII.

1. What do you think (about) every day? 2. I think of something about the books (*shomotu no koto wo*). 3. Do you go to see a picture to-day? 4. No, I go to see the flower. 5. Did you receive my letter yesterday? 6. I did not receive your letter yesterday. 7. Did you hear an amusing story last night? 8. Yes, I heard an amusing story last night. 9. What did you

read yesterday morning? 10. I read an amusing book yesterday morning. 11. Did you not see the beautiful flowers in Asakusa? 12. I saw the beautiful flowers in Okuyama. 13. What do you drink every day? 14. I drink tea every day. 15. Did you not drink saké last night? 16. I drank saké last night. 17. Did you dislike the garden of Asakusa? 18. I did not dislike it. 19. Did you make that beautiful cabinet (*tedansu*)? 20. Yes, I made that cabinet. Do you like (it)? 21. Yes, I like (it). 22. Have you not seen this picture yet (*mada*)? 23. No, I have not seen (it) yet. 24. What (*dō*) do you think of that? 25. I think that good (*yoi to*).

CXIII.

Oide nasaru koto ga dekimasu,   can go.
Oide nasaru koto ga dekimasen,   cannot go.
Oide nasaru koto ga dekimasita,   could go.
Oide nasaru koto ga dekimasenanda, could not go.
Teduma, conjuring. | *Katana,* sword.
Tedumasi, conjurer. | *Karuwaza,* acrobatic feats.
Odori, dancing. | *Karuwazasi,* acrobat.
Wuta, song. | *Hebitukai,* snake tamer.

In conversation, the relative pronoun is not used. For instance, *Kore wa watakusi ga yomimasita shomotu de gozarimasu.* This is the book I read.
. . . . *to yuwu* . . . . called. For example, *Sumi-*

Japanese and English Exercises.

da to yuwu kawa, a river called Sumida, *Tokio to yuwu mati,* city called Tokio, &c.

Gei, acting, or art.
Gedai, the title of a play.
Yekaki, painter.
Awarena, sorrowful or touching.
Sansui, landscape.

Tokoro, scene or place.
Yakusha, actor.
Hanasika, storyteller.
Koshakusi, lecturer.
Kadi, blacksmith.
Kenbutunin, spectator.
Nadakai, famous.

1. *Miyoniti anata wa sibai ye oide nasaru koto ga dekimasu ka.* 2. *Hei, watakusi wa iku koto ga dekimasu ga doko no sibai ye anata wa oide nasaru ka.* 3. *Watakusi wa miyoniti Asakusa no sibai ye ikimasho.* 4. *Nan to yuwu sibai no gedai de gozarimasu ka.* 5. *Tiwusingura to yuwu gedai de gozarimasu.* 6. *Sono sibai ni wa awarena tokoro ga takusan gozarimasu ka.* 7. *Tiwusingura ni wa takusan awarena tokoro ga gozarimasu.* 8. *Nan to yuwu yakusha ga Asakusa no sibai ni orimasu ka.* 9. *Danzurō to yuwu yakusha ga orimasu.* 10. *Danzurō wa watakusi ga mayeni mimasita yakusha de gozarimasu.* 11. *Konniti anata wa Meguro to yu tokoro ye oide nasaru koto wa dekimasen ka.* 12. *Konniti watakusi wa dekimasen.* 13. *Sakuzitu anata wa karuwaza wo goran nasaru koto ga dekimasita ka.* 14. *Hei, dekimasita.* 15. *Kenbutunin ga takusan orimasita ka.* 16. *Kenbutunin ga takusan orimatita.* 17. *Sono atode* (after that) *nani wo goran nasareta ka.*

18. *Sono atode hebitukai to tedumasi wo mimasita.*
19. *Sono atode oyado ye* (to your house) *okayeri nasareta ka.* 20. *Īye, sore kara mata hanasika to koshakusi wo kiki ni ikimasita.* 21. *Dare ga kono katana wo kosirayemasita ka.* 22. *Sore wa Masamune to yuwu katana kadi ga kosirayemasita katana de gozarimasitu.* 23. *Sakuzitu odori wo goran nasaru koto ga dekimasita ka.* 24. *Īye, odori wo miru koto wa dekimasenanda ga wuta wo kiki ni iku koto ga dekimasita.* 25. *Nan to yuwu wuta wo okiki nasareta ka.* 26. *Yugure* to yuwu wuta wo kikimasita.*

CXIV.

1. Could you go to see dancing yesterday? 2. No, I could not go to see dancing yesterday, but I saw a snake-tamer. 3. Did you come home after that? 4. No, I went to (see) a theatre after that. 5. What (*Doko no*) theatre did you go to? 6. I went to a theatre in Asakusa. 7. What is the name of the play? 8. It is a piece called Awanonaruto. 9. Is it amusing? 10. No, it is touching. 11. Could you go to the place called Ozi yesterday? 12. Yes, I could go (there). 13. Could you not go to see conjuring yesterday? 14. No, I could not go to see conjuring, but I went to see (some) pictures. 15. What pictures did you see yesterday? 16. I saw landscapes. 17. Who painted

* "Twilight."

them? 18. A famous painter called Hokusai painted them. 19. Where do you go to-day? 20. I go to hear a story-teller. 21. What story (*Nan to yuwu hanasi*) are you going to hear? 22. I am going to hear the story of Tiwusingura. 23. Who is the story-teller? 24. I do not know (his) name. 25. Tiwusingura is the story I heard before.

CXV.

Where two or more verbs are connected by the conjunction "and" in an English sentence, the verbs in a Japanese sentence change their termination except a final one, in order to avoid the repetition, of *masu, masen,* &c. For instance, *Watakusi wa Asakusa ye ite, hana wo mite, sore kara kayerimasho.* I shall go to Asakusa, see the flower and then return. Here the words *iku* "to go," and *miru* "to see," are respectively changed into *ite* and *mite.* These forms of the verbs remain the same whether the tense is present, past, or future.

Where a verb is governed by a relative pronoun in an English sentence, the verb in a Japanese sentence often changes its termination. For instance, *Sore wa watakusi ga mita shomotu de gozarimasu,* That is the book (which) I have seen. Here the verb *miru* "to see," is changed into *mita.* The following is the declension of the verb ending in *ku*.

Iku, to go,	Ite. / Ita.
Hataraku, to work,	Hatarite. / Hatarita.
Nabiku, to incline,	Nabite. / Nabita.
Taku, to burn,	Taite. / Taita.
Kiku, to hear.	Kite. / Kita.
Aruku, to walk,	Aruite. / Aruita.
Tataku, to beat,	Tataite. / Tataita.
Nageku, to mourn.	Nageite. / Nageita.
Kaku, to write or paint,	Kaite. / Kaita.
Maneku, to beckon,	Maneite. / Maneita.
Toku, to solve, or dissolve,	Toite. / Toita.
Yaku, to toast, or burn,	Yaite. / Yaita.
Hiku, to draw, or pull,	Hite. / Hita.
Naku, to cry, or weep,	Naite. / Naita.

Japanese and English Exercises.

Tuku, to stab, { Tuite.
                { Tuita.

Sirizoku, to retire, { Sirizoite.
                      { Sirizoita.

✓ 1. Kore wa Kanaoka ga kaita ye de gozarimasu ka.✓ 2. Iye, sore wa Hokusai to yuwu yekaki ga kaita ye de gazarimasu. 3. Watakusi wa kono tegami wo kaite okurimasu. 4. Watakusi wa sore wo ite mimasho. 5. Sore wa watakusi ga kīta hanasi de gozarimasu. 6. Watakusi wa sono koto wo kīte kanasimimasita (lamented). 7. Watakusi wa mainiti hataraite hi wo okurimasu. 8. Kore wa watakusi ga sakuzitu aruita miti de gozarimasu. 9. Anata wa konniti Asakusa made aruite oide nasaru ka. - 10. Hei, Watakusi wa konniti Asakusa made aruite ikimasu. 11. Sono hito ga kono inu wo tataite korosimasita (killed). 12. Sore wa kono hito ga tataita hito de gazarimasu. 13. Watakusi wa kore wo midu ni toite ye wo kakimasu. 14. Kono hito ga sono neko wo yari (spear) de tuite korosimasita. 15. Watakusi wa miyoniti soko ye ite sono hana wo mimasho. 16. Watakusi wa sakuzitu Asakusa ye ite sono tori wo mimasita. 17. Watakusi wa hataraite kane wo mōkemasu (earn money). 18. Watakusi ga Yokohama ye ikimasita tokini minato ni takusan fune ga orimasita. 19. Kono hito ga sono ami (net) wo hīte sakana wo torimasu. 20. Anata wa Mukozima ye oide nasareta tokini sakura wo goran nasareta ka. 21. Iye, watakusi *ga Mukozima ye ita tokini sakura wa mada gozarimasenanda.*

CXVI.

1. I heard the story and returned. 2. I went there, heard that story, and returned. 3. I shall go there to-morrow, hear that story, and return. 4. When I went to Sinagawa, I saw a large dog in the street. 5. That is the story I heard last night. 6. I went to Mukozima, and saw the flower of the cherry-tree. 7. This man has beaten this dog, and killed it. 8. I shall paint a picture and send it to my friend. 9. I shall burn this stone (*isi*) and make it (or reduce it to) powder (*ko*). 10. This child heard that news and wept. 11. I shall work and earn money. 12. That is the letter I wrote yesterday. 13. That is the book I wrote. 14. I shall write a letter to-morrow and send it to that person. 15. Is this the dog which barked last night. 16. No, that is not the dog which barked last night. 17. Who painted this picture? 18. That is the picture Kanaoka painted. 19. Who sent that picture? 20. My friend painted and sent it to me.

CXVII.

The verbs ending in *au*.

Au, to meet, { *Ōte.* / *Ōta.* }

Japanese and English Exercises.

Tatakau, to fight, { Tatakōte. / Tatakōta. }

Mau, to dance, { Mōte. / Mōta. }

Hau, to creep, { Hōte. / Hōta. }

Nerau, to aim, { Nerōte. / Nerōta. }

Warau, to laugh. { Warōte. / Warōta. }

Kau, to buy. | Sitagau, to obey.
Usinau, to lose. | Utagau, to doubt.

The verbs ending in *mu* and *imu*.

Konomu, to like, { Kononde. / Kononda. }

Nomu, to drink, { Nonde. / Nonda. }

Tutusimu, to revere, or to be reverential, { Tutusinde. / Tutusinda. }

Kanasimu, to lament. { Kanasinde. / Kanasinda. }

Yomu, to read. { Yonde. / Yonda. }

Tanomu, to trust. { Tanonde. / Tanonda. }

Tanosimu, to enjoy. { Tanosinde. / Tanosinda. }

I

114   Japanese and English Exercises.

Kurusimu, to suffer,
{ Kurusinde.
  Kurusinda.

Kabe, wall.
Tuta, ivy.
Meirei, command.
Mise, shop.
Tobu, to fly or jump.
Katāna, sword.

Wakareru, to part.
Sina, article or thing.
Osiye, instruction.
Teppo, gun.
Tuye, stick.

1. Watakusi wa miti de sono hito ni ōte hanasi wo kikimasita. 2. Kono hito wa watakusi ga sakuzitu Asakusa de ōta hito de gozarimasu. 3. Kireina tuta ga kabe ni hōte orimasu. 4. Sakuzitu watakusi ga kōta tokei wo konniti usinaimasita. 5. Kore wa watakusi ga sakuzitu kōta sina de gozarimasa. 6. Watakusi ga teppo de nerōta tori wa tobimasita. 7. Watakusi wa anata no osiye ni sitagōte kono koto wo simosho. 8. Kono hito wa anata no meirei ni sitagōte konniti kono tokoro ye kimasita. 9. Kono hito ga sono hito wo warōte soirimasita. 10. Kore wa watakusi ga sakuzitu usinota sina de gozarimasu. 11. Sono hito wa hito wo utagote sono tegami wo watasimasen. 12. Anata wa kono sake wo kononde onomi nasaru ka. 13. Watakusi wa kononde nomimasu. 14. Kono hito wa mainiti kono tokoro ye kite sake wo nonde tanosimimasu. 15. Kore wa watakusi ga nonda sake de gozarimasu. 16. Sono hanasi wo kīte kanasinda hito wa kono hito de gozarimasu. 17. Watakusi wa sono

sina wo kōte, kono hito ni tanonde, watakusi no tomodati ni okurimasho. 18. *Watakusi wa sakuya hanasika no seki ye ite, omosiroi hanasi wo kīte, tanosinde kayerimasita.* 19. *Kono shomotu wo yonde kurusinda okata wa dare de gozarimasu.* 20. *Sore wa watakusi de gozarimasu.* 21. *Sore wa watakusi ga kono mise de kōta sina de gozarimasu.* 22. *Watakusi wa sono koto wo kīte, tegami ni kaite okurimasita* 23. *Sakuya kono ko wa awarena hanasi wo kīte, nasite, kanasimimasita.*

CXVIII.

1. This is the person I met in the street yesterday.
2. This is the article I bought in the shop yesterday.
3. I shall obey your command and do this matter.
4. Does this person like saké, and drink much?
5. Yes, this person likes saké and drinks much. 6. I bought that article in this shop and sent it to you just now. 7. I went to a story-teller, heard an amusing story, and then returned. 8. This child heard a touching story and cried. 9. What did you see when you went to Asakusa? 10. I saw birds when I went to Asakusa. 11. I wrote a letter and sent it to my friend. 12. What did you write in the letter which you sent to your friend? 13. I wrote an amusing story in my letter, which I heard last night. 14. I suffered, worked, and earned money. 15. That man

has beaten this dog with a stick, stabbed it with a sword, and then killed it. 16. That person met me in the street and (we) parted just now. 17. This is the thing I bought yesterday at Sinagawa. 18. This is the place where I came yesterday. 19. That child heard that story and cried. 20. I went to my friend's house just now and returned. 21. I shall go to this story-teller and return.

CXIX.

Atumeru, to collect, { Atumete. / Atumeta.

Oboyeru, to remember, { Oboyete. / Oboyeta.

Tokeru, to melt.
Miru, to see.
Homeru, to praise.
Kangayeru, to think.

Nigeru, to run away.
Taduneru, to look for.
Okiru, to get up.
Nagameru, to gaze.

The verbs ending in *aru*.

Atumaru, to assemble, { Atumatte. / Atumatta.

Suwaru, to sit down, { Suwatte. / Suwatta.

Hasiru,* to run, { Hasitte. / Hasitta.

* This verb changes its termination in the same way as those ending in *aru*.

Japanese and English Exercises. 117

Kiru,* to cut,	{ Kitte. / Kitta.
Ikaru, to become angry,	{ Ikatte. / Ikatta.
Tomaru, to stop,	{ Tomatte. / Tomatta.
Uketoru,* to receive.	{ Uketotte. / Uketotta.
Uru,* to sell,	{ Utte. / Utta.

The Verbs ending in *uru*.

Kuru, to come,	{ Kite. / Kita.
Bassuru, to punish,	{ Bassite. / Bassita.
Suru, to do, or to make,	{ Site. / Sita.
Hassuru, to start,	{ Hassite. / Hassita.
Tassuru, to reach,	{ Tassite. / Tassita.
Hossuru, to wish, or to intend,	{ Hossite. / Hossita.

* These verbs change their termination in the same way as those ending in *aru*.

118 Japanese and English Exercises.

Hei, army.
Noti, future, or after.
Na, name.
Yo, generation.
Kō, Lord, or a term of respect.
Seifu, government.
Wasureru, to forget.

Yubin kiyoku, post-office.
Yubin, mail, or post.
Tuini, finally.
Minato, harbour.
Mukasi, ancient times.
Ikusa, battle.
Makeru, to be defeated.

1. Kono tokoro wa mukasi Hideyosi kō ga hei wo atumeta tokoro de gozarimasu. 2. Yubin wa itu kono minato wo hassite itu Osaka ye tassimasu ka. 3. Kono yubin wa konniti kono tokoro wo hassite miyoniti Ossaka ye tassimasu. 4. Sono zainin wo bassita hito wa dare de gozarimasu ka. 5. Sono zainin wo bassita hito wa seifu de gozarimasu. 6. Watakusi wa tadaima tegami wo kaite yubin kiyoku ye okurimasita. 7. Sakuzitu anata wo hometa hito wa kono hito de gozarimasu. 8. Mituhide wa Yamasaki ni hei wo atumete Hideyosi to tatakōte tuini makemasita. 9. Masasige kō wa Minatogawa no ikusa ni utizini wo site noti no yo ni na wo nokosimasita. 10. Watakusi wa sono hanasi wo kīte, oboyete, hito ni hanasimasho. 11. Yuki ga tokete, kawa no midu ga masimasita (increased). 12. Kore wa watakusi ga sakuzitu uketotla tegami de gozarimasu. 13. Kono inu wa naite orimasu. 14. Watakusi wa kosikake ni suwatte, shomotu wo yonde, tanosimimasu. 15. Watakusi wa kono tokoro ni tomatte miyo asa ka-

yerimasho. 16. *Watakusi wa miyoasa hayaku okite, sitaku wo site, kayerimasho.* 17. *Sono hito wa kono tuye wo katana de kirimasita.* 18. *Shomotu wo yoku yonde kangayeta hito wa yonda koto wo wasuremasen.* 19. *Watakusi ga taduneta hito wa sono hito de gozarimasu.* 20. *Kono hito wa kokoni atumatte sore kara dokoye ite, nani wo simasu ka.* 21. *Kono hito wa kokoni atumatte, hanasi wo kite tanosimimasu.* 22. *Maiban watakusi wa kono tokoro ye kite, kireina hana wo mite tanosimimasu.* 23. *Kono hito wa shomotu wo yonde, sore wo oboyete, sosite hito ni hanasimasu.* 24. *Kono tegami ga tassite, sono henzi* (reply) *wa itu kimasho ka.* 25. *Sore wa miyoniti kimasho.*

CXX.

1. Who punished that criminal? 2. The government punished that criminal. 3. Is this the place where Hideyosi collected his army? 4. No, this is the place where Yosimoto collected his army and fought against Nobunaga. 5. What is this place called? 6. This is the place called Okehazama of Narumi. 7. Do you stay here and amuse (yourself)? 8. Yes, I shall stay here, see this place, and then return. 9. Why do these people assemble together here, and where do these people go? 10. These people go to a story-teller's house and hear the story. 11. I shall consider this matter (*koto*) and do it. 12. When does this mail start from

this harbour and reach Yokohama? 13. The mail will start from this harbour to-day and reach Yokohoma to-morrow evening. 14. I met that person in the street and told that story. 15. I bought that article in this shop and sent it to my friend. 16. Is this the place (where) I have lost a knife, and looked for it yesterday. 17. Yes, this is the place where you have lost your knife. 18. Is this the name of a person who came here yesterday? 19. Does this child read that book and remember (it) well. 20. Yes, that child reads that book, remembers it well and tells the other people what he has read (*yonda koto*). 21. Did you receive this letter and read it yesterday? 22. I received this letter yesterday and read it this morning. 23. Did you hear an amusing story yesterday, write it in a letter, and send it to your friend? 24. Yes, I wrote in a letter an amusing story which I heard last night, and sent it to my friend.

www.ingramcontent.com/pod-product-compliance
Lightning Source LLC
Chambersburg PA
CBHW021939160426
43195CB00011B/1155